PRAISE FOR *FINDING MR. RIGHTEOUS*

"With an entirely fresh perspective and a voice that's humorous, hopeful, and, at times, absolutely heartbreaking, Lisa De Pasquale's quest to find Him is a must-read. I loved *Finding Mr. Righteous,* agonizing over the rough patches along with De Pasquale and cheering her on throughout, and I can't recommend this book highly enough!"

—JEN LANCASTER,
New York Times bestselling author of *The Tao of Martha*
and *Here I Go Again*

"Lisa De Pasquale is one of the best conservative writers out there, but this book isn't about politics. It's a fascinating and extremely personal account of her dating life, her massive insecurities and her mostly ineffective search for God—until one man accidentally reveals the truth to her. I won't tell you how, or I'd ruin the ending. This is a true Christian story, disguised as racy 'Chick Lit.'"

—ANN COULTER,
New York Times bestselling author and columnist

"*Finding Mr. Righteous* is a true page-turner that will touch many lives. That's because it's a very sharply told, sometimes hilarious, sometimes sordid, but always bravely honest account of one woman's search -- in all the wrong places—for connection, meaning, peace, and true love. By refusing to sugar-coat the sorrows and humiliations of her wanderings, her journey's end is all the more wonderful, powerful, moving, and sweet."

—ERIC METAXAS, *New York Times*
bestselling author of *Bonhoeffer: Pastor, Martyr, Prophet, Spy*

FINDING
MR. RIGHTEOUS

FINDING
MR. RIGHTEOUS

{ Lisa De Pasquale }

A POST HILL PRESS BOOK

A POST HILL PRESS book

ISBN (hardcover): 978-1-61868-9-818
ISBN (eBook): 978-1-61868-9-825

Finding Mr. Righteous copyright © 2014
by Lisa De Pasquale
All Rights Reserved.

Post Hill
PRESS

Published by Post Hill Press
109 International Drive, Suite 300
Franklin, TN 37067

Cover design by Ryan Truso
Supplemental design by Travis Franklin
Interior book design by Neuwirth & Associates, Inc.

Visit us online at http://posthillpress.com

CONTENTS

I have been all things unholy.
If God can work through me,
He can work through anyone.

—ST. FRANCIS OF ASSISI

FINDING
MR. RIGHTEOUS

PROLOGUE

It was a Saturday afternoon when I realized I was using religion to get a guy. I had spent an hour crafting the perfect message that he would respond to in his trademark witty prose. Or was it that I was using a guy to get religion? Were my questions about religion real and my lusting after him fake? As I began to think about my past relationships, I thought about my private journey to find God. Some brought me closer, others drove me further way. This book is about the men I've met on a quest to know Him. Even as I write this, I don't know how my story will end. Will I find my soul mate or save my soul? Is it too much to ask for both?

CHRIS
the Atheist

1

I was on the metro coming back from a Candye Kane show. Candye was a porn star-cum-lounge singer. I adored her because she was sexy, a big girl like me, and she embraced it, unlike me. I stood there surrounded by her mostly male fans and I started to feel a little sexier. After she finished her set, she came off stage, made a beeline for me, and gave me a big hug. I was glad that I ended up going to the show even though I had to go alone. It's not every day your music idol gives you an unsolicited hug.

After the concert, as I waited on the platform at the Clarendon metro station, two guys asked me if they were going in the right direction. In a drunken stupor, they had previously taken the train in the wrong direction. It was already past midnight, so this was their last chance on a Thursday night to get it right.

We boarded the same train and I walked toward the middle and sat in an empty row. After a few minutes, I noticed one of the guys looking my way. The other guy was cuter, and it sounded like he had an Australian accent. The American walked toward me and sat down in my row. We exchanged names. His name was Chris.

"Where were you tonight?" he asked

"A concert," I said.

"Who did you go with?"

"No one. Just by myself."

"You went by yourself?"

"Yeah, I really wanted to go and no one else I knew wanted to go."

"That's cool."

I rolled my eyes to myself. This guy was drunk. When guys have nothing to say, they say, "That's cool."

"You seem really drunk," I said.

"Yeah, I'm not used to drinking that much," he said.

"Oh."

"So, do you want to go with us to get breakfast?"

"No, thank you. I need to get home."

I'd heard of these male-female encounters, read about them in magazines, but this had never happened to me before. I'd never been "picked up." I wasn't really sure how to react. Was this guy just making conversation? Surely he wasn't just looking for a one-night stand, because he would go after someone who was hot, right? I just sat there being amused by his every drunken word.

"You're funny," I said.

"You're pretty," he said. He reached across my chest and brushed my hair out of the way, which was loosely falling in between my cleavage. "Will you give me a kiss?" he asked.

"I don't know you."

"Please?"

So I did. A peck, really. The first thought that came to my mind was that there was an old Asian man sitting in front of us who must have figured out we didn't know one another before getting on this train. Now he just saw me kiss a total stranger.

"It's almost my stop. Can I have your phone number?" he asked.

I gave him my number. He got up and walked back to his friend on the other side of the train.

A few minutes later, Chris came lumbering back.

"I can't stop thinking about that kiss. Can I have one more?" he asked.

Now that I was more aware of the other people on the train, I said, "Only on the cheek." I gave him a quick peck. The train stopped and Chris and his friend got off.

It was around 2:00 p.m. on Sunday when the phone rang. I looked at the caller ID. It must be the guy from the metro, I figured. I decided to play it cool and not pick up. Since it was Sunday, I wanted to watch some football anyway. A few hours later, the phone rang. It was Chris again. This time I picked up.

"Hello?"

"Hi, this is Chris from the metro."

"Oh, hi, how are you?"

"I'm good. I called you earlier, but I guess you weren't home."

"Oh, yeah. The Redskins game had just started, so I didn't pick up."

"That's cool."

Ugh. He later told me that ignoring him in favor of the football game was what made him decide he really did want to see me again.

I live in Herndon, Virginia, which is about twenty-five miles northwest of Washington, DC. Since my job is also in Herndon, I really don't venture out of the suburbs that much. One night, though, I was going with my friend Christie to a bar called Zed's in Alexandria. Chris and I had talked on the phone a few times, so I decided to invite him along since Zed's was near his apartment. When we showed up, he was wearing a polo-type shirt with a weird pattern. I had forgotten what he looked like. He kind of looked like Patrick Swayze in *Dirty Dancing*.

He seemed really uncomfortable. We were surrounded by Christie's libertarian friends, who still thought it was cool to argue about politics after work. I realized how pretentious they seemed when I brought someone new into the mix. Maybe that's why I noticed his ugly shirt. It reminded me of a guy I worked with in college who used to wear similar collared shirts with golf balls and tees on them. He was really cool and the shirts didn't fit his personality. One day I asked him if he played golf. He said he didn't.

"Then why do you always wear golf shirts?" I asked him.

"My dad gave them to me. Clarence said we have to wear collared shirts when we're working at the counter, and these are all I have."

That's when I realized how little guys think about what they wear. Shirt plus pants equals dressed.

At around 9:00 p.m., Christie said she was ready to leave. Chris offered to take me home if I stayed while he finished his beer. We left about ten minutes later. He had a white Chevy truck. When he opened the door, he quickly moved all the paper, fast-food bags, bottles, and random guy garbage that accumulate in all of their vehicles.

"Do you know how to get to your house from here?"

"I know you just need to get on 495 and take it to the toll road," I told him, privately annoyed that he didn't know how to get around the area.

"We could just go to my house."

"No, I have a dog and I need to let him out," I said.

When we got to my house, my dog, Buster, greeted us at the door. "Does he always jump like that?" Chris said.

"He's just excited that I'm home."

"You have a really nice place. Too bad it's way out in the boonies."

"It's not in the boonies. It's near where I work."

"Boonies," he said, smirking.

I figured he was teasing me to be cute, but it was annoying.

"Are you tired?" he asked.

"Yeah, kind of."

"Can I stay here tonight so I don't have to drive all the way back to Arlington?"

Oh. So, this is where the boonies conversation is going. "Let's watch some TV for a while," I suggested.

We sat on my couch and Buster jumped up on his lap. He pushed him off.

"Don't push him!" Seeing his reaction to my sweet, sweet dog trying to check him out should have been my first clue that Chris had a dark side.

That night we slept in the same bed, fooled around, but didn't, you know, sleep together. I slept in shorts and a tank top in mismatched pastel colors. I was going for cute, not trying too hard to be sexy. I knew I wasn't sexy, but it would be worse if it seemed like I was trying to be sexy and failing. Buster slept in the spare bedroom. I secretly wished Buster and Chris could just trade places, but I didn't want to seem like a crazy dog lady on our first date.

2

Chris and I had been dating for about two weeks. We hadn't had sex yet. I told him I didn't go that far so soon. It was mostly true. I had really only had three boyfriends. The first I never slept with and was the first boy I ever kissed. The second was my first and it was awful. The third was my first real relationship. I broke it off with him on Valentine's Day because I knew after I graduated from college I wanted to move to DC. He offered to come, but that was a turnoff for me. Anyone willing to move a thousand miles for me obviously didn't have much going on in his own life.

I was at Chris's apartment one night. We were fooling around on his adolescent twin bed with no frame. Earlier that day I had heard "Landslide" by Fleetwood Mac on the radio and I couldn't get it out of my head.

"I have a song in my head. Have you ever heard 'Landslide'?"

"Wow, I've had that same song in my head, too."

I slapped him on the chest. "No way. Are you serious?"

"Yes! I swear. That is so amazing. I can't believe you said that song."

I realized how late it was and that I had to get home. My car was at the metro near my mom and stepdad's house. They were watching Buster because I hated leaving him home alone. Chris said he was hot and was going to change clothes, so I left the room while he got dressed.

I was waiting in the living room when he came out in cargo shorts and a heather-grey James Madison University T-shirt. It was tight on the top and showed off his chest and biceps. I had never noticed his body before because he wore those awful ill-fitting golf shirts. Holy shit, I was dating a hot guy.

A week later we slept together. We were at my house. I had made him wait for three weeks. After we were done, I jokingly said, "See, that wasn't such a big deal." I thought I was being cute, but he was offended. He went outside to smoke for a while. I never knew where I stood with him.

Since I was living in the" boonies," we usually only saw one another on the weekends and talked on the phone during the week. We were talking one night and he seemed distant. I could hear him chain-smoking and grabbing a bottle out of the fridge. I knew what was coming.

"I don't think we should see each other anymore," he said.

"Why?" I asked.

"I don't want to get into the reasons. It's just for the best."

"Is it because of my looks?" I asked. I thought this would throw him off. Make him feel sympathy for me. In a million years I wouldn't have expected what he said next.

"Yes."

I didn't get mad. How could I blame someone for thinking the same thing I thought about myself? I needed to lose weight. That didn't change just because a guy showed mild interest in me.

"I was planning to lose weight anyway," I told him. "Why don't we continue dating and see how it goes? Or are you just embarrassed to be seen with me?"

"No, I don't care what other people think."

When we hung up that night, we were still dating. The next day I bought the weight-loss book *Body for Life*.

As the weeks went on, my phone conversations with Chris got more and more deep. We were about a month into dating. It was a week-night and I was getting ready to go to bed when Chris called. Once again, I didn't know where the conversation was leading.

We started talking about religion. Chris often made off-hand comments about being an atheist, so I was surprised when he told me he grew up in a Pentecostal church. It was the kind where people talked in tongues when they felt the spirit. He said he would sit in the pew and wish he could hear the voices. I said maybe they were all faking it. I was surprised when he said they really heard them. He asked me what I believed. I said that I believed in God. I grew up Southern

Baptist, though I was never really that religious. I just knew I wasn't an atheist or agnostic.

"So, you can't even defend your beliefs?" he asked.

"Well, it's better than being a heathen like you!"

"Do you really freaking think that? I can't believe you would even say that to me."

"I was just kidding; I didn't really mean it," I stammered.

"Then why did you say it? You're saying I'm someone who deserves to go to hell."

"I swear I didn't mean it that way."

"I wouldn't wish hell on my worst freaking enemy. If you really think that about me, we have a problem."

I could hear the sneer in his voice.

"I don't. I wasn't thinking. I guess I'm just sort of scared that you're making me realize that I don't really believe in anything. Maybe I don't even believe in any religion."

"But you believe in one that will send me to hell."

"What do you mean? There's always forgiveness," I said.

"Not for blasphemy. You have to accept that if God is real, we're both going to hell."

I didn't know what to say. I knew I didn't have enough knowledge of Christianity to defend it or condemn it. He was right. At that moment I felt my heart harden. I couldn't defend God, and I definitely couldn't argue with Chris and still keep him.

"Lisa, there's something I have to tell you. I don't want you to interrupt me."

"OK. I'm sorry."

"Lisa, I love you. I mean it. I really do."

Once again, Chris had caught me by surprise. He said, "I love you." All I had to do was renounce God.

3

Chris and I frequently imagined that our life together would be better without the stress of our jobs, DC area traffic, and the DC area cost of living. Chris had spent a few years in North Carolina and reasoned that it would be a better place to live and raise a family.

Since 9/11, we frequently talked about getting away from the area. Both my mother and Chris were working in the Pentagon on 9/11. I was flying to Florida that day when a flight attendant announced that all planes were being grounded because of a national emergency. The first thought that came to my mind was that the president had been assassinated. Once the plane landed at the nearest airport in Columbia, South Carolina, the flight attendant announced that planes had hit the World Trade Center and the Pentagon. I grabbed my cell phone and immediately called my mom. To my shock, I got through. She was fine, but still at the Pentagon. Then I called Chris. Given that I was on a plane and had no access to the news, I had no idea how serious the situation was at that point. When Chris answered, I jokingly said, "How's your day going?"

"Are you freaking serious?" he said.

"I'm still on the plane. I don't really know anything."

"They're saying it's terrorists. I got the hell out of there. A cop stopped me on the way home for speeding. The Pentagon is on fire and I get pulled over for speeding. I told him I was coming from the Pentagon and to just give me the ticket so I could get home."

"Wow, that's crazy," I said.

"Listen, I can't talk right now. I need to process what's going on."

"OK, I guess I'm not going to make it to Florida, so I'll probably rent a car and drive back tonight."

"OK," he said as he hung up.

I knew when to not push him to talk. Certainly, that moment was one of those times. It didn't even occur to me that Chris hadn't tried to call me. Or that he didn't ask about my mom or how I was feeling.

In November 2001, we rented a cabin in the mountains for a few days. I found a great place on Craigslist. It was a beautiful log cabin just a few yards from a stream. "Cabin" really doesn't do it justice. It was two stories, with a Jacuzzi in the master bedroom and a wraparound porch with beautiful views of the surrounding area.

When we arrived at the cabin, we realized we were about forty minutes from the nearest grocery store. After bringing all of our stuff inside, I noticed the "house rules" on the refrigerator:

- No smoking in the house
- Place dirty sheets and towels in laundry basket before leaving
- No smoking in the house
- Empty refrigerator before leaving
- Leave check on the counter
- *NO SMOKING IN THE HOUSE*

I was delighted to see that I would be able to enjoy a weekend free of secondhand smoke. It made my eyes water, gave me headaches, smelled horrible, and made everything I wore smell horrible.

"Did you see the rules?" I asked.

"Yeah, no smoking. It's not a big deal, I'll just go outside."

I sighed with relief. It wasn't just about my personal discomfort but that he was willing to put effort into doing something that was good for both of us.

After getting settled, we drove the forty minutes into town to the closest grocery store. We loaded up on things that would last us several days and that didn't require much cookware since I forgot to take stock of what was in the kitchen. I enjoyed cooking for Chris, so I was looking forward to doing several days of meals for us. It also gave me something to do while he was outside smoking.

The next day we attempted to go fishing. The cabin owners told us it was too late in the year, but we tried it anyway.

That evening I filled up the Jacuzzi and grabbed a book. Even though it was "built for two," I was too modest (or ashamed) to actually use it with Chris. He didn't ask to join me either. After a long bath, I got dressed and went downstairs where Chris was watching TV. There he was, sitting on the floor, a few empty beer bottles strewn about and a makeshift tinfoil ashtray. He was smoking. In the house. He lasted less than twenty-four hours.

"You're smoking?"

"It's OK, we'll just open all the doors before we leave and air it out," he said without looking at me.

I was tempted to tell him what a soulless, insensitive asshole he was. It's what I should have said. In reality, I said nothing. I went back upstairs to go to sleep.

A few minutes later, Chris came upstairs and laid down in bed with me.

"What's wrong?" he asked.

"I don't understand why you just can't stop smoking. You know my dad had so many health problems from smoking. How can I be with you knowing you're risking your health the same way?"

"I'm sorry, baby. I didn't know it hurt you that much."

He was drunk. That's the only time he ever called me "baby." The truth was, I wasn't upset because of the health risks. I was upset that he didn't have the self-control to not smoke inside for a few days. If he couldn't do that, he couldn't control his other impulses either. His impulse to drink. His impulse to be so cynical about the world. His impulse to leave me because I wasn't thin.

The next morning when I woke up, Chris was lying next to me. His leg was resting on mine. It reminded me of the joke about the difference between cats and dogs. A dog will lay next to you because he wants to be closer to you. A cat will lay next to you because you're warm. Chris was a cat. I knew the morning intimacy was accidental. But I was starving for it. I didn't want to move. Even though I was dying to use the bathroom, I stayed in bed until he woke up.

4

Don't get me wrong, I didn't renounce twenty-plus years of personal religious beliefs just because I was dating an atheist. My ambivalence about religion had started much earlier. Even at nine or ten years old, I knew there was something that didn't connect me to a particular religion. My mother, sister, and I were attending a Southern Baptist church in Tallahassee, Florida. It was in a nicer neighborhood than where we lived. One Sunday I decided it was time for me to be baptized, or "born again." Baptists believe that after birth, a person should choose to get baptized again in order to show their true commitment to their faith.

I didn't feel the call that I thought I was supposed to feel, so I faked it. As my mom busied herself with unlocking the car door, making sure my sister was strapped in, I pretended to be preoccupied. When she told me the door was unlocked, I ignored her and looked off into the distance. Later I said I couldn't stop thinking about all the fire and stuff in hell.

I began on the path of getting baptized. It happened during a Sunday evening service. The regular pastor wasn't there, so one of the deacons did the baptism instead. He was tall, bearded, and had reddish-brown hair. Afterward I joked that when I was coming out of the water, I thought he looked like Jesus. Later, I received congratulations from members of the congregation. There was no mistaking me because I was the only one with wet hair.

Chris and I were still dating after almost a year.

Being with him, I also became more and more cynical about religion. I don't know if it was an effort to show him how much I had changed, or if my heart was just getting harder after enduring months of his disapproval.

Some nights he would call me and say he loved me more than he'd loved anyone. That he would die for me. I would tell him that a statement like that was more about him not caring about his own life.

On weekends we would do our weigh-ins. Whoever lost the most would have to pay for lunch on our "free day." Most of the time it was me who had to pay. I figured it was a sure bet to get us to spend time together, because he wouldn't turn down a free meal.

On Sundays I would buy groceries and make him meals for the rest of the week. Grilled chicken, roasted potatoes, chili, breakfast casserole. I would be in the kitchen most of the day; he would be at the computer playing chess and watching football. If there was a good play, he would call me to come watch. It made me happy knowing that I was useful to him, especially since I was no longer being asked to perform other "girlfriend duties."

We started doing the Body for Life program in order to lose weight. My progress was slow. Too slow, he told me. He would call me late at night and say he couldn't continue dating me, but then he would tell me I always managed to say the right thing to keep him from fully breaking up. I noticed he was drinking and smoking more than ever. I hated the smoking, but I should have been more worried about the drinking. One night he confessed that he didn't use to drink this much. He said since he met me, he started drinking more because I made him feel guilty. "You're the best girl I've ever known," he said, "and I feel so guilty that I'm not attracted to you. You deserve better than me."

I responded that I just wanted to make him happy. Didn't he want to be happy?

One Saturday night in May, I was getting ready to go out with Chris and some of his friends when he called. He said it was over. The acoustic version of Staind's "It's Been Awhile" played on the radio.

Why must I feel this way?
Just make this go away.
Just one more peaceful day.

I collapsed on the bed and cried. He called a few nights later. I said I would continue losing weight and wait for him.

5

Nearly six months had passed since I last saw Chris. We still e-mailed or talked on instant messenger every day and on the phone at night. He was dating a girl named Danielle. I was working out for an hour every day and eating eight hundred to a thousand calories. I wanted to give myself a goal, so I bought tickets to a Wizards-Lakers basketball game and asked if he would go with me. I knew he wouldn't pass up the lineup: Michael Jordan had just started playing for the Wizards and Shaquille O'Neal and Kobe Bryant were playing for the Lakers.

I took the metro into DC that evening, eager to see if Chris would notice a difference in the way I looked. I was wearing a sleeveless black dress from Old Navy. It was formfitting, but flattering.

After some confusion over which metro exit was closest to the restaurant where we were meeting, I finally saw Chris on the sidewalk. We walked toward one another. I looked at his face for a sign whether he could tell how much weight I had lost——approximately sixty pounds. We hugged one another and I couldn't stop myself from asking, "Do I look different?"

"Yeah, you look good."

As we ate dinner, we talked about our jobs. He was still doing computer work; I was still with a nonprofit group. My career was actually starting to pick up. I was writing more, doing more talk radio interviews, and booking more speakers on college campuses.

We had nosebleed seats for the game, but the view was still pretty good. I'm not a basketball fan, but being able to see some of the modern-day greats on the same court was cool. About halfway into the game, Michael Jordan went out because of a knee injury. As it would turn out, that was the last professional game he ever played.

Later that night we found ourselves on the metro together again. His stop came first. We were on a crowded train, so I knew there wasn't going to be a declaration of love or regret, but I was still hoping for something. I smiled. He said, "It was good to see you." As much as I wanted some sort of affection then, I can't remember if we hugged good-bye.

For months I couldn't stand the name "Danielle." I built her up in my head as the perfect girl who was happy with her body, could motivate Chris to stop drinking and smoking, who did fun things with their mutual friends on the weekend. Chris and I never did anything with mutual friends. He once went on a weekend trip to go inner-tubing with some friends at work. He didn't even invite me. I reasoned that it was because he knew I wouldn't go tubing because I would be afraid of the water or of being in a bathing suit in front of other people. Either way, it was my fault, not his.

I did know there was one thing I could give Chris that no one else could give him: unconditional love and understanding. He told me so. One night while we were still dating, he told me about his horrible family life. After his mother and father got a divorce, she married a horrible man who physically abused him and his sister. It was worse for his sister. Chris asked me if I ever noticed the marks on his arms. I hadn't. After his mother and stepfather were divorced, he found out about the physical abuse his sister had endured. He began cutting himself on his upper arms every day. There were dozens and dozens of scars on both arms. He couldn't stop his stepfather, but he thought he could at least feel his sister's pain. The next time I had the chance to look at his arms, I was shocked I hadn't noticed before. It was typical of our relationship. I never thought about his flaws because I was obsessing over my own.

I continued to lose weight and was soon down almost ninety pounds. My gym posted "before" and "after" photos of me at the registration desk. I was starting to get attention from guys, which confused me. I'd been overweight since I was four years old, so I wasn't used to getting male attention.

A flirtation started with the UPS guy who had my office's route when the regular guy was on vacation. We talked on the phone and eventually got together one evening. I made him spaghetti and meat-balls. He confessed that he was legally separated from his wife, but they still lived together.

I met another guy while I was getting new tires and we started to date. He was Indian. He had been in an arranged marriage, but once his parents realized it wasn't working they gave him their blessing to get a divorce. He wanted to spoil me. It was new and I liked it. One evening at a restaurant, he drew on the butcher paper on the table the house we would live in, the car he would buy me (a Lexus), his car, and our weekend car. We only dated a month. He insisted that I give him back a necklace he gave me. The request was so petty that I wanted to be sure he knew I didn't care about any of the things he had given me. I gathered the necklace, every empty vase from flowers, a teddy bear, perfume, and anything else and put them in a garbage bag. I gave them to his best friend so I wouldn't have to see him.

I also bought my own Lexus a few years later.

Chris and I still talked, though. He always insisted that I was the one. That we were the only ones who could make each other happy. One night he invited me over to see his new apartment. He said he and Danielle were no longer dating. On my way out, I grabbed the mail. I had received the new Victoria's Secret catalog, so I took it along in case I got bored watching Chris play chess and smoke.

When I arrived, Chris was surprised at how good I looked now. He couldn't stop looking at me, and for the first time I felt like I had power in our relationship. He said he and Danielle were still friends and he still had her stuff there. We started fooling around and he seemed nervous. Afterward, I went to take a quick shower and opened a nearby closet to get a towel. On the floor was an Avenue bag. Avenue was a frumpy, plus-size store. Danielle was fat.

When I got out of the bathroom, Chris was on the phone. He hung up, turned to me, and said, "Danielle is on her way over."

"What?" I said.

"She had a hard day at work and just needs someone to talk to for a few hours. I'm sorry."

"So, you want me to leave?"

"Yeah, I'm sorry."

I was out the door in less than five minutes. I was in shock. I told myself they were just friends. I smirked when I realized that I had left the Victoria's Secret catalog behind. She would at least know I had been there. Of course, a normal woman with some self-respect would have picked up the catalog and threw it at him.

The next morning I didn't see Chris on instant messenger. This was a bad sign. Chris frequently called in sick when he was torn up inside. I romanticized it, but in all honesty he was probably hungover from a night of heavy drinking and smoking.

I called him at home. Danielle was still there. They were getting back together.

"Were you ever really apart?" I asked. "Does she know I was there last night?"

"Yeah, she knows. We're going to get married."

I hung up and sat there in shock. How did I lose again? I was skinnier now. She was fat.

A few days passed and I sent Chris an e-mail. I didn't understand, I told him. I had lost the weight. What had changed? Wasn't I better now?

He wrote back, "I'm sorry. It's also the hair on your face. I know there's nothing you can do about it. It just bothers me."

I wish I could say that at that moment I realized what a jerk he was, but I didn't. I responded that I knew I had facial hair and I had been researching electrolysis, but couldn't afford it right then.

From that day forward, the weight started to come back. My religious beliefs, to the extent that I ever had any, didn't.

6

Chris and I frequently talked about having children. I always said that the one thing I wanted to accomplish in life was to be a stay-at-home mother. Even after we broke up (or the last time we broke up), Chris would e-mail me that he still thought I would one day be the mother of his children. In my mind, I had added up all our similar beliefs on having children, not believing in organized religion, wanting to get out of DC—even having the same song on our mind meant that we were meant for one another. There was never a time that I turned him away. Even when I knew I didn't have the same feelings for him, I didn't want him to think I had rejected him.

After not speaking for several months, maybe even a year, he asked if he could call me. He told me he and his ex-girlfriend Heather had a baby and named her Chloe. They had broken up but had sex one last time. Even though she was nearly forty, she got pregnant. I wanted to ask if Chloe had been baptized.

I was now the director of the nation's largest conservative political gathering, writing regularly and getting paid for it, and he still ended up on top. He ended up with the prize I wanted.

Over the years Chris and I loosely kept in touch. Every eight to ten months or so, one of us would make contact. Usually it was him when things weren't going well in his life.

Chris moved to Richmond, Virginia, to be closer to his daughter. For a few months he had a temporary job in Falls Church. One day out of the blue he e-mailed and asked if I wanted to get dinner and see his place. I had plans to get a drink with a board member at my organization, but I said I would meet him at his hotel and then we could go to dinner.

When I arrived, I was surprised at how different he looked. He had gained weight and now had a goatee and glasses. When we started kissing, it was the first time I didn't feel anything. It reminded me of when I was at a conservative event where a prayer was said before dinner. I practically reveled in the fact that I didn't feel anything.

I realized at dinner that I was a totally different person around Chris when we dated. Back then I was afraid of being funny because I was afraid of his criticism. When I said something funny during dinner, he was surprised. I rarely made him laugh, even though I tell people that one of the things I'm looking for in a husband is someone who laughs at my jokes.

Chris liked to reminisce about one particular night we spent together at his apartment. He lived four stories up and there was a balcony off the living room. We were out there one night while he smoked and drank. I didn't know if he was drunk or just already so completely comfortable around me that he didn't care about doing the gross guy behavior they're supposed to hide for a few months. He started spitting from the balcony to see how far it could go. I laughed along with him as his spit went further and further. It was disgusting. I wasn't amused. And I'm still annoyed that his favorite memory of our time together was like a scene from a gross-out teen movie.

Most of my memories from our relationship involved being alone or ignored. Chris was an avid chess player. He would drink, smoke, and play online for hours. I would sit there watching TV or reading a book. After a few months he taught me how to play. I was a quick learner and even won my level at a chess tournament we went to in Fredericksburg. Well, he remembers that I won. I remember that we slept in different beds that night—although it was better than my usual sleeping spot at his house, the floor, because he only had a lumpy twin mattress.

After several months of not speaking, I heard from Chris a few days before Halloween. He was back in Richmond. He had bought a house but was still looking for a full-time job. He asked if I would come down for a visit to see his place. Still unable to say no when I thought he needed me, I drove down Halloween evening. It was still light when I got there and he showed me around the backyard, holding my hand, proud of the random things that were growing in his garden.

It started to get darker, so we went inside and he showed me around. He may have had a house, but it looked like every place he'd ever had. Nothing on the walls, not much furniture, cluttered with makeshift ashtrays, beer bottles, and dirty dishes. This time it was clear: there was no woman living here. I also couldn't imagine his young daughter of four or five being here.

After several years of wanting Chris to be attracted to me, I didn't mind when he tried to get me in the bedroom after less than an hour. I didn't want to do anything with him, I just wanted to be wanted.

Chris had already been drinking. His eyes were droopy and he wasn't very engaged when we talked. When we were last together, he said that another ex-girlfriend, Mariah, liked it when he got rough. But I didn't expect what happened next.

As we were kissing on his bed, he pulled away, reached back, and slapped me hard across the face. I was shocked. He hit me so hard I actually saw stars. He acted like it was totally normal. Maybe it was for him.

Later that night I said we could watch the TV show *Profiler*. I had just gotten the first season because a friend of mine was in the show. After five minutes, he became fixated on the main actress. He couldn't stop talking about how she'd probably never struggled a day in her life because she was pretty. Without asking, I got up and took the DVD out. He went back to playing chess on the computer.

Ten years had passed and we were in the same roles. Except I wasn't. It wasn't that I had become less insecure; it's just that I had gotten older and had less patience for Chris's negativity. I told him I was going to head back to Northern Virginia so I wouldn't get home too late.

As we started saying good-bye, Chris broke down and started sobbing.

"You know, my dad died. I didn't think I'd take it this hard."

"I'm so sorry."

He came toward me and I hugged him. He started crying in my arms. I felt nothing but annoyance. I never knew when Chris was having real emotions or had just drank too much. Chris's father was an alcoholic. As far as I know, they had only seen one another a handful times since his parents got a divorce when he was a child. He frequently talked about being a better father to Chloe than his father had been to him. The bar was set pretty low.

Chris and I never talked about the fact that he was also an alcoholic. Maybe he doesn't think he is. I've heard him say a hundred times that he's drinking less or going to drink less. When we were together, I never saw him drink less. At the beginning I thought it was my fault. He told me he had to drink in order to be with me. He said he felt so guilty being with me because I was so good and he was a just piece of shit.

It was New Year's Eve of 2001 when I realized how much he really drank. It was the middle of the night when I felt a tug on the sheets. I opened my eyes. The lights were on and Chris was stripping the bed.

"What's going on?" I asked. The second I spoke, I realized one side of my pajamas was soaked. I looked back at him and just said, "Oh." Chris had been so drunk that he urinated in his sleep. All over himself and all over me. I got up, changed my clothes, and didn't say a word about it. Ever. I didn't want to embarrass him by calling attention to it. It was always about his feelings. Even when I was literally getting pissed on, I wanted to protect him from any more pain in his life.

When he didn't have a job, when his father died, in between getting back together with Heather or whatever woman was in his life, he would reach out to me. In December 2011, he sent me a message on Facebook:

> I never stopped loving you or your body. You are beautiful inside and out. And nobody could ever love you like I love you. I think you should give me another chance. I could just hold you. That would be good enough for me. Just let me hold you. I will always love you, Lisa. No matter what.

After nearly twelve years of this back and forth, I finally realized that he just wanted to know that there was someone like me out there for him. In the twenty-four to forty-eight hours it took to talk myself into letting Chris back into my life, his communication would drop off. This usually meant that he was back together with whoever he was dating at the time. In later years, the rejection didn't hurt at all. It was more of an annoyance.

Finally, after more than a decade of putting his feelings first, I cut off all contact. He had mentioned in a subsequent e-mail that he got a new phone and didn't have my phone number. We had mostly been communicating on Facebook over the last two years, so I blocked him. One day he might come across my e-mail, but for now he is out of my life.

I spent a lot of time and energy on a relationship that would never work. I also lost a relationship I spent no time on. I lost a relationship with God, albeit a passive one. Did I pray every day before I met Chris? No. But, I wasn't the cynical person I had seemingly become. I reasoned that if I could gain anything from the time I spent with Chris, it was that he taught me the truth about religion. I would steel myself against God. I dared God to show himself to me. He didn't call my bluff. Wasting twelve years of my life had a purpose if I held on to the belief that Chris taught me to outgrow belief in God. If I held on to that, it wasn't for nothing.

JOE
the Catholic

7

Every year, thousands of conservative activists from across the country gathered at a hotel in Crystal City, Virginia. There were panels, dinners, awards, and political speakers. No one under thirty cared about any of that, though. For them, the conference was about meeting people. Several years prior, a liberal journalist wrote about the conference as if it were some sort of sex-filled orgy. He wrote about Caligulas in khakis who moved hotel minibars from multiple rooms into one home base of sex, drinking, and business card sharing. There was just one problem. The chairman of the conference noted in his response to the magazine's editor that the hotel didn't have minibars. The editors started asking the reporter questions and his story began to unravel. It turned out he had made up details and taken things from other stories and eventually left in disgrace.

The conference is where I met Joe. Truthfully, we had seen one another at meetings around town, but the first time I ever really talked to him was when he stopped by my organization's booth in the exhibit hall. He worked at a communications consulting firm in Old Town, Alexandria. He had a goatee. A lot of guys in DC had goatees at that time. It was like they were all rebelling against the fact that they were getting closer to thirty and basically had desk jobs. DC life was more like *Office Space* than *The West Wing*.

"Hey!" he said.

"Hi there," I said.

"What's going on?"

"Some crazy guy is passing out fake pornographic photos of one of our speakers. He put them at everyone's booth," I said.

"Do you need help?"

"I don't know. We went around and picked up a lot of them."

"Let me know if I can do anything to help."

"OK, thanks. Oh, you can help me get a picture with the Ultimate Warrior!"

"I'm on it," he said.

He walked away and I didn't think much about him the rest of the weekend. I did get a photo with the Ultimate Warrior, though.

Chris and I were done, but I still worked out every day. I was starting to gain back some weight because I was actually eating now. When I was losing weight for Chris, I would sometimes be physically unable to eat. I would take a bite of a bagel and couldn't even enjoy it because all I thought about were the calories. For a week I ate almost nothing but that one blueberry bagel.

It was Sunday and I was at my friend's gym because my gym was closed on Sundays. The gym was near her apartment complex's 's business center was also near the gym, so I stopped by to check my e-mail on the way out. There was an e-mail from Joe, the guy from the conference. It was a forward for an outing at a nearby winery. Typical. This was how DC guys operated. Rather than actually ask a girl out on a date, they would forward an e-mail to a happy hour or some other function. It's not a date invitation, so there's no fear of rejection by the guy. Girls don't know what to do with this sort of passive invitation. Does it mean he wants to go together? Since it's just drinks, should I plan for dinner afterward? I have to go straight from work, so should I wear that wrap dress that accentuates my waist to work? Or should I change at work? But what if I see someone at the happy hour that I saw during the day and they notice I changed into something different? The happy hour e-mail is simply a transfer of anxiety.

I decided to take a stand. I wrote back:

"I don't really know much about wine. Why don't you take me to dinner instead?"

The second I sent it, I worried I was totally reading the situation wrong. Who was this post-Chris person writing this e-mail?

A few minutes later, I got a response from Joe:

"Ok. How about Thursday?"

I smiled. I had broken the cycle. Maybe I was no longer the insecure girl I used to be. Maybe now I was in control.

On Thursday, Joe picked me up and we went to a nearby Italian restaurant. I ordered balsamic chicken and Joe got eggplant parmagiana.

"Are you a vegetarian?" I asked.

"No, I just gave up meat for Lent."

"Oh, that's Catholic, right?" I said.

"You're an Italian girl. Aren't you Catholic?"

"Well, I was originally baptized Catholic, but I was baptized again in a Southern Baptist church. I've never been to a Catholic mass."

I didn't want to mention that I had given up on God or thought that by now God had given up on me. Definitely not first date talk. "So, does that mean you can eat meat on Friday since you don't eat meat the rest of the week?" I asked.

He laughed. "No, I have to be good the whole week."

"Do you ever go by Joseph?"

"No, I'm a Joe."

We talked throughout dinner. He was easy to talk to and thought I was funny. He was practically the opposite of Chris in every way. His mother was Hispanic and his father was Jewish. He was from New Jersey. Also, he drove a Jeep, which was kind of hot.

Afterward, Joe walked me to my doorstep. We had a quick kiss.

"Do you want to come in?"

"Of course!"

I smiled and grabbed his hand. Buster promptly sat right in between us on the couch like a chaperone. After a few hours, we went upstairs. Sleeping with a guy right away was not my nature and as comfortable as things seemed with Joe, that night wasn't an exception.

Early in the morning, just before the sun came up, I woke up and looked at Joe. He was lying on his back and smiling.

"What are you smiling at?" I asked.

"Nothing, I'm just happy," he said.

I looked out the window and saw a few inches of snow on the ground.

"Yuck, it snowed!" I told him.

He reached across me to pull back the curtain and look. "That's not snow. That's just a dusting."

"It's enough that I have to clean off my car before driving."

It was Friday morning, so we still had to go to work. I jumped in the shower while he slept a little longer. When I came out of the bathroom he was gone. I looked out the window to see if his Jeep was still there. There he was, cleaning the snow off my car with his bare hands.

I went downstairs as he was coming in the front door.

"You cleaned off my car!" I exclaimed.

"Just the windows and top so you can drive," he said.

"Thank you! You made my day."

"What are you doing this weekend?"

"I don't know, probably nothing."

"Do you want to come to a basketball game with me? My old college is playing."

"Sure, what college did you go to?"

"Catholic."

Of course he did.

"Sure, that could be fun."

"Cool, I'll e-mail or call you and we'll figure it out."

We kissed and he left. I was giddy the rest of the day.

By the time I got to work, I already had an e-mail from Joe. He suggested we meet at his place because the basketball game was in DC and he lived in Alexandria. Even though we had only gone out on one date, it felt good to know where I stood.

On Saturday I met Joe at his place. I was pleasantly surprised. Unlike Chris, he had a "big boy bed" (not two twin mattresses on the floor) and even had some art on the walls. In a single guy's apartment, anything framed counts as art. Even cartoon superheroes.

When we got to the game, the inner fat girl in me panicked when I saw that the gym had the standard wooden bleachers. Falling on the bleachers is painful enough, but being the fat girl who falls on the bleachers in front of a gym full of college kids would be beyond humiliating.

We went about halfway up and I proclaimed, "This is a good spot!"

I'm not much of a basketball fan, but I was enjoying being with Joe and him including me in his life. On the second date we were already light-years ahead of me and Chris.

"I'm kinda disappointed that your mascot is a bird and not an actual cardinal," I said.

"What are you doing tomorrow?"

"Nothing. Maybe go to my friend's gym since mine is closed. Why?"

"Because I wanted to see if you want to get dinner before I have to meet a friend for a movie."

"Sure. That works."

On Sunday Joe came by my house and we went to a nearby Greek diner. Talk turned to sex, and I asked the question girls aren't supposed to ask.

"So, how many girls have you been with?"

"Eight. And you?"

"Twice that. Wait, no I mean half that. Four." So, I thought, I either sounded like an idiot or a slut. (For the record, the number really was four.)

"Either one is OK with me," he said.

"Do you have time to come back to my house before your movie?" I asked.

"Sure. I don't have to meet Allison until eight."

"Allison?" I said, trying to sound breezy.

"Yeah, a friend from college."

"Is it like a date?"

"No, we're just friends."

"I've heard that before."

I didn't want to have the uncomfortable "Are we dating exclusively?" conversation. We went back to my place. We slept together for the first time. Since Joe had evening plans, he didn't hang around very long.

"Have fun on your date," I said as he reached for the door.

"Don't say that. It's just a movie."

The situation was too familiar. I didn't blame Joe for leaving. I knew he had evening plans, and it was my idea that he come back to my place. Making the comment about his "date" was a defense mechanism. If I acknowledged it, maybe it wouldn't be true. Or if it was true, he'd tell me right then or feel guilty.

He kissed me and left.

8

It was fun dating someone who was involved in the conservative movement. Actually, I should say it was convenient dating someone in the movement. So often I would have to go to a conference or meeting and not know anyone there. With Joe, I had a plus one.

In April, one of the largest conservative think tanks was holding its annual conference in New Orleans. Joe and I were both being sent by our employers. It would be my first time going to New Orleans as an adult. I wanted to do the touristy things, and Joe came up with a list of things we had to do. Beignets at Café Du Monde, po'boys, muffulettas, Hurricanes at Pat O'Brien's, crawfish, Bourbon Street.

We weren't able to get on the same flight, so Joe arrived about an hour earlier. We took a cab over to the hotel, where we each checked into our own hotel rooms. I was still working for a very conservative womans' organization, so I had to keep up appearances.

The conference didn't get underway until the next day, so we decided to take a quick nap before venturing out. I went to Joe's room. It was too early for pajamas and too uncomfortable to be in regular clothes, so we got undressed and got under the covers. An hour later I woke up. My head was on Joe's chest. I had drooled on him. He didn't seem to mind. It was one of the most comfortable moments I'd ever had in a relationship.

When I was with Chris, I developed an addiction to sleeping pills. I couldn't sleep without them. When we were dating, I was self-conscious about what I looked and sounded like when I slept. On more than one occasion, he woke me up to tell me that I was snoring. His only concern was that he get back to sleep before I could get back to sleep and start snoring again. When we weren't dating, he would interrupt my sleep at all hours of the night by calling. He was always drunk and vulnerable, so I felt like I had to talk to him. If I didn't, all the worst things he thought about himself would be true.

But with Joe, I fell asleep in his arms, I drooled on his chest, and he didn't complain.

It was April in New Orleans and unseasonably cool. I hated everything I brought to wear. Since it was a work trip, I only brought work clothes and nothing for a casual stroll along Bourbon Street. It was dark, which meant the drunks were already out. Since it wasn't Mardi Gras, I thought all the Marci Gras clichés wouldn't apply. Not ten minutes into our stroll did we see a group of rowdy guys surrounding two girls, egging them on to lift their shirts. Witnessing this stone-cold sober disgusted me. I averted my eyes and kept walking. I looked to my left and was surprised to see that Joe had joined the crowd. I patiently waited for him while seething inside. I didn't want to seem like a jealous girlfriend (was I even his girlfriend?), so I didn't say anything. I was already over Bourbon Street.

Joe was set on making sure we did the must-do activities in New Orleans. Our first stop was for a Hurricane at Pat O'Brien's. A photographer came around taking souvenir photos, so I bought one. It was our first photo together.

After a full day of conference activity, Joe insisted we go for crawfish for dinner. We settled on a restaurant near the hotel that didn't have a long wait. Joe didn't even glance at the menu.

"You have to eat crawfish," Joe said over a plateful of them.

"No, thank you," I said.

"We're in New Orleans. It's the law."

"I don't like to eat something when I can see its face."

"But you can't. See, you pull off the tail, then suck it. The face isn't looking at you."

"That is so gross."

"You're missing out!" he said.

"You're sweating."

"It's spicy."

"Then I definitely don't want one."

"Wimp."

We went back to the hotel and did what two twentysomethings do in a hotel in New Orleans. Later that night, I had a really uncomfortable burning . . . down there. Lesson learned about dating someone who likes spicy food.

Things were good between me and Joe. Not serious, but good. Any time I tried to engage him in a serious discussion, he defaulted to the good-natured guy routine. There were no late-night declarations of love like there were with Chris. There were no declarations at all. Even though I called him my boyfriend to friends and family, I didn't refer to him as my boyfriend in front of him. Even though I felt like I knew how he felt about me, I was still apprehensive about letting him know how I felt about him.

One Saturday we went to my neighborhood pool to lay out. I was reading my friend's new book defending Joseph McCarthy. Joe was reading the new *Harry Potter* book. We made a good pair. So much so that a local newspaper reporter took our photo for a feature on summer reading.

We went to my house and before showering, we had sex in the middle of the day. I was more physically open with Joe, but still emotionally closed. I gave him glimpses, like insisting I didn't want to go out on Friday nights because I had to work out on Saturday mornings. The truth was that Joe was more outgoing. He wanted to mingle and talk to people. I wanted to spend time with him. Or at least avoid making small talk with people. Joe liked to network, which is DC-speak for drinking with people in the same career field as you.

The summer was ending soon, which meant it was almost Joe's birthday. He was turning thirty. I started to see the first signs that Joe was not the happy-go-lucky guy he showed the world.

"Are you excited about your birthday?"

"No, I'll be old," he said.

"You'll be older. You're already old."

"Thanks."

"What do you want for your birthday?"

"I don't want anything."

"That's no fun."

"Really, I don't want anything."

"What about thirty presents for your thirtieth birthday?"

"Fine, thirty presents is the only thing I want."

So, that's what I got him. They were mostly small, quirky items like a toilet paper dispenser that played "Love Me Tender" when it moved (his bathroom had an Elvis theme) and an "Al Sharpton for President" T-shirt.

Joe and I did things that couples did. I would stay at his house and then we would drive in together to political meetings we both had to attend. We tried new restaurants. We went to shows. We met one another's parents. We bickered in a playful way. He even took me to a Catholic mass once. But we never talked about a future together or our feelings for one another. He never said he loved me and I never said I loved him. I thought I might one day, but I was determined to not be in the same kind of one-way relationship I was in before.

The one time Joe took me to church, it was to the chapel at his alma mater. It was my first Catholic service since being baptized as a Catholic as a baby. Needless to say, I didn't remember the various prayers and recitations. I felt awkward not knowing when to stand and when to mumble along with everyone else. There are Christmas and Easter Christians and then there's me, the baptism and funeral Christian. I had no idea what was going on, but the incense was a nice touch.

Any time I tried to engage Joe about his religion, he made a joke. I often wondered why he wasn't as insistent as Chris that we have the same beliefs. I assumed it just meant he was more open-minded than Chris the Atheist. Imagine that.

Most of what I knew about Joe's religion was from the outside. He would offhandedly say he was going to Bible study. When he said it was at a bar, I was confused. Bible study was supposed to be in an overlit church basement and led by a guy in a sweater-vest who might be gay. It made less sense than Christian heavy metal. (Yes, it exists.)

I asked him one day, "Why don't you ever take me to church?"

"I did!"

"One time! At Catholic University!"

"You didn't really seem interested."

"But don't you want me to be better?"

"That's more of an evangelical thing. I'm Catholic. This is what I believe, and you're welcome to come if you're into it."

I wanted to be pursued, though.

One Valentine's Day, Chris had greeted me at the door and quickly said, "Sorry, I forgot. I don't have anything for you."

Yes, Valentine's Day is just a way to sell cards, candy, and flowers. It's also a way for guys to make up for their thoughtlessness the other 364 days of the year. But in this relationship, I wasn't looking for romance. I didn't expect any guy to have those strong feelings for me anyway. My relationship with Joe was always more playful than romantic.

"Do you want to do Valentine's Day presents now?"

"Sure," he said.

I handed him an envelope. "I got us tickets to a romantic movie."

He opened the envelope and smiled.

"It's got passion!" I said.

Inside the envelope were two tickets to the opening of *The Passion of the Christ*.

"Good job," he said. "Now it's time for you to get ready for where we're going."

"Where are we going?"

"It's a surprise."

"How do I know what to wear?"

"You don't need to wear anything fancy."

Then I did something I started doing soon after we met—reaching into his front shirt pocket and pretending to be disappointed that nothing was there. Eventually he started putting things in the pocket. Usually silly things, like the fifty-cent toys you get in vending machines in grocery stores. Today I reached into his pocket and there was a plastic card. I pulled it out and it was a gift card to Dave and Buster's. My eyes widened. "Is this my surprise? I've always wanted to go there!"

"Maybe."

"I'm so excited! Thank you!"

"I just said maybe."

Spending Valentine's Day at a place with my dog's name in the title was perfect. He even gave me all the game tickets he won, which was pretty romantic in my book.

I realized we had been dating for nearly a year when Lent rolled around again.

"Why do you always give up more than one thing at Lent? Don't most people just stick with one thing?" I asked.

"I'm an overachiever," said Joe.

"What are you giving up this year?"

"Alcohol, meat, and sex," he said.

Um, what?

"Is there anything left?" I asked.

"I just want to see if I can do it."

I wanted to ask "What about me?" but I knew that's not what the cool, casual girlfriend would do. It was only forty days anyway.

One night we were at his apartment and watching a movie. I playfully started rubbing his leg, going higher and higher.

"Stop it. I'm not doing that right now," he said.

"So, you have that much willpower?" I said as I continued teasing him.

"Why can't you just respect what I'm doing?" he said, a little too angrily.

I was humiliated and embarrassed. I walked out of the room and went to lie on his bed. A few minutes later he came in.

"What are you doing?" he asked.

"I'm going to bed since there's no reason to stay up."

"What's the matter?"

"You just made me feel like a whore that no one wants!" I said into the pillow

"I didn't mean it like that. I just don't want to do that stuff right now."

I couldn't say what I really wanted to say. What the cool, casual girlfriend doesn't say. Sex is not just sex. Sex is confirmation that a guy is attracted to me.

I hadn't always been that way. I've always had a self-esteem issue when it came to my looks, but dating Chris brought it to the forefront. I thought I had left that part of me behind when Joe and I started dating, but here I was again. I was willing to forgive his flaws, but he wasn't willing to forgive mine.

A few weeks later we went to the opening of *The Passion of the Christ*. I turned away for a good part of the movie. I couldn't watch all of the violence. The movie itself was good. It even had some quirky aspects. Apparently, Jesus invented the modern-day dining room table with chairs.

When the movie ended, the lights came on and it was obvious that Joe had been crying. He knew he would always be forgiven.

I don't remember when I first met Joe's parents. I think it had been the previous summer. They were visiting DC. Joe met my mom and stepdad at Thanksgiving. We were going through the motions of being a couple. In April, my stepsister and her husband were in town consulting for a musical that was playing at Ford's Theatre—*Children of*

Eden. Joe's parents were going to be in town the same weekend, so my stepsister got tickets for all of us to go to opening night.

We took our seats and immediately Joe and I are started acting like two siblings fighting over the armrest. We teased each other.

My mom said, "The two of you are just alike the way you pick on each other."

Children of Eden is a musical based on the book of Genesis, telling the stories of Adam and Eve, Cain and Abel, and the Flood. It's never been on Broadway, but the cast that night deserved to be. The musical weaves together these stories with a character called "Father," an on-stage embodiment of God. It was amazing.

"You know, this counts as going to church," I said to Joe after the show was over.

"For you it does," he said.

We all walked to the nearby Gordon Biersch brewery and restaurant for dessert. Our families sat at different tables because we didn't have reservations for a larger table. My mom thought we acted like kids, but I felt like it was the most grown-up relationship moment I'd ever had in my life.

9

That summer Joe decided to leave his job at a tech-centered communications firm and go to a public relations firm. One of the bonuses was a weekend away for an ad sales presentation sponsored by a DC newspaper. The weekend was at Keswick Hall, a resort near Charlottesville, Virginia. We were given a nice suite with a balcony that looked out on to the golf course.

Lent was over, but the no sex rule was still in effect. I had also gained back most of the weight I lost when I was with Chris. Joe never said anything about it.

When we arrived at Keswick, we were told that we could have our pick of two amenities. We picked a spa treatment and horseback riding.

We got settled in the room. While Joe took a nap, I went on the balcony and called my sister. A few minutes later Joe came out.

"You're talking really loudly," he said.

"Sorry, I didn't think you could hear me."

"You're outside. Everyone can hear you."

"OK, geez," I said, rolling my eyes.

We had been on our weekend getaway for less than an hour and we were already getting on each other's nerves.

The next day there was a pitch meeting Joe had to attend in the morning. I got a facial and then we met up to go horseback riding in the mountains.

The owner of the stable brought out two horses. They were huge. Had I never seen a horse up close, or were these freakishly large horses? Joe got on his horse with no trouble. I spent an hour crying and shaking because I was terrified of this animal. I eventually got on the horse and stayed on for about thirty seconds. It was too high, and I knew riding up and down the mountain trail would be too much for me.

The next day there was nothing on the schedule, so I wanted to grab a quick lunch and then spend the day at the pool. Joe wanted to go into Charlottesville, which was about forty minutes away, to some sandwich shop.

"Why can't we eat at the clubhouse here?" I asked.

"Because there are better, cheaper places in Charlottesville."

"But it's forty minutes away. After going there, eating, and then coming back, the day will practically be over! I want to spend time by the pool."

"Well, I don't want to eat at the clubhouse. Why are you being so difficult?"

"I'm not being difficult; I'm telling you what I want to do."

"No, you just want to fight."

"I don't want to fight. I want to go to the pool. I don't care about lunch, so go get your sandwich. I'm going to the pool."

Somehow during my tantrum, I managed to gather my poolside accessories (book, sunglasses, towel, hotel key, etc.). I think I even put my bathing suit on. That's multitasking only a woman can do. Then I left the room. It occurred to me that this was something I never would have done with Chris. I was so afraid of him getting mad at me. With Joe it was the opposite. I wanted him to get mad. Prove that he actually cared about our relationship. Did we even have a relationship, or were we just two people that did stuff together? It was starting to look more like the latter.

Once I got to the pool, I found a good lounge chair facing the sun and started to read. Twenty minutes or so passed before Joe came and sat on the chair next to me.

"What are you doing?" he asked.

"Reading," I said without looking at him.

"Do you want to go get lunch?"

"No, I'm not hungry."

"We can go to the clubhouse."

I sighed. He still didn't get it. I didn't have a preference on the place but on the time allotted. It wasn't worth the energy.

"OK."

Things were still tense during lunch. Joe's allergies were bothering him, which I suppose was one reason he didn't want to spend the afternoon outside.

"It always seems like you're sick with something," I said.

"Why are you being such a bitch?"

I overplayed my snarky hand.

"I just mean your allergies are really bad. Isn't there a stronger medicine you can get that's not over the counter?" I asked.

"I don't know, probably. They've always been bad."

We were reduced to an old couple talking about health issues. I figured any minute we'd start discussing whether the tomatoes were good that year.

Our weekend at Keswick was over. As we drove back to Northern Virginia, things got serious.

"I'm just not happy with my life right now," Joe said.

I couldn't help but think of what he said the morning after our first day together. He was happy then.

"So what are you going to do about it? You just started a new job. Isn't that going well?"

"I'm not talking about my job. I'm talking about my life. I don't think you're happy either."

I didn't realize at the time he wasn't talking about himself or me. He was talking about "us."

A week after we got back from our weekend at Keswick, we had to start making plans for the Republican National Convention in New York. Finding a hotel for less than $500 a night was out of the question. Even though I didn't have a convention pass, there were lots of opportunities to do some media for my organization and attend the infamous convention parties I had heard about.

"When are you going up?" I asked.

"I'm going to see my family for a few days beforehand," he said.

"Oh, I can't go up that early."

"Just take the train up."

"By myself? I have no idea where to go. I don't even have a place to stay yet."

"I'm staying with my friend Danielle."

Seriously? I thought. *Another Danielle in my life?*

"Is it near where everything is?" I asked.

"It's within walking distance or a short cab ride. She has room for two."

"I'm just wondering if it would be too crowded. Aren't New York apartments really small?"

"That's where I'm staying. If you don't want to stay there, then you'll need to do some networking to find a place to stay," he said.

He was clearly annoyed with me. He never actually said it was OK for me to stay at Danielle's. I was already on my own getting there.

"OK, count me in if it's OK with her," I told him. "Will you meet me at the train station since I'll have no idea where I'm going?"

"Yes, I can meet you there."

We hadn't talked at all about our conversation on the way back from Keswick. We still e-mailed and talked on the phone. The PR firm he was working for set up several radio and TV slots for me. It was a busy week before the convention, so we didn't see one another until I arrived in New York.

When I got off the train at Penn Station, the first thing I noticed was that there were police everywhere. It was beautiful. Thankfully, I managed to find the right exit and saw Joe among the crowd of NYPD officers, convention goers, and pissed-off commuters.

"I made it."

"You made it," he said.

"So, do we need to get a cab or something?"

"No, I can pull your suitcase. It's just a few blocks away, near Times Square."

When we arrived at Danielle's apartment, she was still at work. I was pleasantly surprised to see that it was pretty spacious. It was a one bedroom, but it had two bathrooms and a den. The den wasn't a private room, but it had a daybed with an additional twin bed that pulled out underneath.

"OK, so what's the plan for tonight?" he asked.

"Well, I got us all on the list for R— The Party. The one the Bush twins are supposedly throwing. We just need to meet up with my friend since she put us on the list."

I was saving my favorite new top for the party that night. It was supposed to be the one attended by the conservative Hollywood folks. Or it was at least rumored that some famous people would be there. The top was sheer and teal, with embroidery and beading. I paired it with black tuxedo pants and strappy sandals.

When Danielle arrived, I realized that we had met before when she lived in DC. She was nearly a foot taller than Joe, which was comforting to my ego somehow. The three of us went to dinner before heading to the party. My feet were killing me before the check came.

After dinner we took a cab to my friend Elizabeth's place. *This* was the typical New York apartment I had imagined. It was on the fourth floor, had no elevator, and was a studio shared by two people. My feet were killing me, so I borrowed Elizabeth's size 10 flip-flops even though I wore a 7.5. I was going to what was supposedly the hottest convention party wearing comically big flat shoes that made my tuxedo pants drag on the ground.

Once we got to the party, everyone seemed to split up. Joe went to the bar to get drinks while I awkwardly stood by myself in the dark club. The party seemed to be comprised of junior staffers and College Republicans. The Bush twins smartly were in a balcony, separated from those who thought they scored a ticket into an exclusive party. I was disappointed. Then Ric Flair, the wrestler, walked by and my hopes were raised.

After ten minutes or so, Joe found his way back to me. "It's not open bar."

"That's surprising. Oh well. You didn't get anything?" I asked.

"I'm not going to pay for drinks at a convention party."

"So, do you want to leave?"

"No, I want to talk to people. Walk around and network."

"I don't know anyone here." Stephen Baldwin walked by. Eh, second celebrity sighting, I guess.

"That's why you have to walk around. Don't just stand in one place."

Danielle came up to us. "I don't think there's anyone here over twenty-five."

"Do you want to hit another party? I think there's another Association of something doing a party nearby," Joe said.

"Not really. I'll just do another lap and then we can leave. Can you believe it's a cash bar?" Danielle said as she walked away.

"Walk around and talk to people," Joe told me. "You look weird just standing there."

"If you wouldn't keep leaving me I wouldn't be just standing here," I said.

Then, to disprove my theory of how awkward I was in social situations, a girl walking by stopped and said, "Oh my god, I love your blouse!"

I smiled and told her thanks.

"See? People want to talk to you."

"No, she was just giving me a compliment. The fact that I'm wearing an awesome top does not overtake the fact that I don't know anyone and no one knows me."

Danielle came back and said, "OK, are you two ready to go?"

"I am!" I said.

We took a cab back to Danielle's apartment. I changed into my pajamas. Joe stripped down to boxers and his undershirt. We crawled into our separate beds and went to sleep.

The next day the convention was underway. I had a few radio interviews in the morning that I was able to do by phone. Joe watched some of the convention on TV. Thanks to my agoraphobic tendencies, I was getting cabin favor. I decided to drop off the tuxedo pants I had worn the night before at the dry cleaners. Given my body issues, I tend to rely on a small number of pieces that I know work for me.

"Can you e-mail Danielle and ask her if there's a same-day dry cleaners she uses that's nearby?"

"Why? You have an entire suitcase full of clothes," he said.

"I know, but I want to wear these tomorrow for my TV interview."

"Just wear something else."

"Listen, don't worry about it. I'll find a place and get us some lunch."

"I don't need lunch. There will be plenty of food at the parties tonight."

"OK, then I'll get myself lunch now and not eat tonight," I said on my way out the door.

For over a year, Joe and I got along very well, but now it seemed like every conversation was tense. What did he care if I wanted to wear the same pants twice during our trip? Or pay for a meal during the convention?

I found a dry cleaner right around the corner that would have my pants done by 5:00 p.m. that day. I also stopped by a deli and got us both sandwiches and chips.

When I walked backed in the apartment, I went to the kitchen to unload the food.

"I got two sandwiches. If you don't want it, someone can eat it later."

"I said I didn't want anything."

"And I said you don't have to eat it. What's the big deal?"

"You never listen to me when I say I don't want something."

"Why are you making such a big deal about it? We're not going to any parties until later tonight. I want to eat lunch. I'm not making you do anything."

An hour or so later he ate the sandwich. And the chips.

It was the first big night of convention parties. Joe had a long list of parties and was hell-bent on hitting as many as possible. We had an early cocktail party at Rockefeller Center. The famous bronze statue of Prometheus was smaller than I thought. This was my first trip to New York since I was ten years old. Everything seemed bigger then. In fact, New York was bigger then. The Twin Towers were still there.

Our next stop on the party circuit was at a famous private yacht club. It was sponsored by several DC-based conservative groups, so there was a good chance I might see a familiar face or two. When we walked in, I was pleased to see that your typical DC gathering of conservatives was transplanted to New York. The first person I saw was Stacie, the director of the conservative conference where Joe and I met. She was also Joe's first boss. We exchanged gossip about the convention and the people who weren't there. We also got the scoop on the big party the next night since Stacie's group was one of the sponsors.

The party was very different from the one the night before. I realized it was because it wasn't trying to impress a New York crowd like R——The Party had been. None of us were from New York. There was no pressure to make it the best party of the week. I had my first mojito! It was already a step above the cash bar from the previous night.

Unfortunately, it wasn't enough for Joe. He was ready to move on to the next party.

"Why do we have to go if this is a good party and we're talking to people here?" I asked.

"Because it's the convention. The whole point is to go to as many parties as possible," he said.

"I thought the point was to have fun."

"I told people I would go to this party."

"Well, I don't want to stay out late because I have that TV interview in the morning. I'll just take a cab back to the apartment and you can go to the party," he said.

"You don't know where you're going."

"Then tell me Danielle's address and I'll just tell the cab driver."

"I'll just take the cab back with you and then go to the other party."

"OK," I said. This wasn't turning out to be the trip to New York with my boyfriend that I thought it would be. Joe seemed more interested in checking off a list of parties than spending time with me. I enjoyed being with him. Talking with him. He was enough for me; why couldn't I be enough for him?

We got a cab. It dropped me off at Danielle's apartment and we said good-bye for the evening.

Less than an hour later, I got a text from Joe.

"This party sucks. You were right."

He was back at the apartment not too much later.

"Why do you want to go to every single party?" I asked him.

"I want to take advantage of everything while I'm here," he said.

"I just think if I'm having a good time at one party, why should I leave?"

"But you're not getting out and meeting new people. You don't talk to anyone."

"Maybe it's that people don't talk to me! I'm tired of talking about this," I said.

I grabbed my pajamas and toiletry bag and locked myself in the bathroom. I didn't want to cry, but I did. He had hit a nerve. The truth was that I was never comfortable in crowds or social situations. After a year and a half of dating, he should have known it by now. Bringing it up made me even more self-conscious about it. I looked at myself in the mirror. The longer I looked, the weirder my features looked. Big nose. Chipmunk cheeks. Too-full lips. Big, oily forehead. Tears started to fall. Add bloodshot eyes to the list.

There was a knock at the door.

"What are you doing?" Joe asked.

"Nothing. Getting ready for bed," I said, trying to compose myself.

"Can I come in?"

I opened the door and tried to busy myself at the sink to mask the tears.

"What's wrong?" he asked.

"I'm not good at networking or talking to people I don't know. Why can't you just accept that?"

"You're funny and charming and fun to be around. I wish you would realize how wonderful you are."

But I didn't feel wonderful. One of us had to be wrong, and I was the one that knew me better. I couldn't continue this conversation anymore.

"Will you just let me get ready for bed? I'm fine. I'll be out in a minute."

I decided to take a long shower, hoping Joe would be asleep by the time I was done. Also, it was the best way to muffle my crying. I didn't believe what he said about me. Joe was the type that wanted to make anyone happy. He had to just be saying those things so I would do what he wanted me to do.

When I got out of the bathroom, the lights were out, but Joe was watching TV. I threw my stuff on the suitcase and got into the top bunk of the daybed.

"Are you going to bed now?" Joe asked.

"Yes."

"What time do we need to be up for your TV interview?"

"I have to be there by ten. I have the address. I can just take a cab."

Joe didn't respond. I pretended to be asleep by the time he turned off the TV and hit the sheets.

The next morning, Joe and I both took a cab to the Warner Brothers studios for my short interview on the role of the next potential First Lady. Could there be an easier topic than the differences between Laura Bush and Teresa Heinz Kerry?

I was glad to see that the camera would only be filming me from the shoulders up. I was wearing a black wraparound top, black pants, and a necklace made of chunky red stones. A production guy came over to mic me up.

"I really like your necklace," he said.

"Oh, thanks. I thought a bright color would look better on TV with the black," I said.

"Yeah, it looks nice."

Then he proceeded to touch the necklace, approximately two inches from my cleavage. It was more intimate than Joe and I had been in months. I looked around to see if he was in the studio. He must have stayed in the green room.

When we got back to the apartment, we watched a few of the convention speeches before heading out to two parties. The early one was at the Plaza Hotel and hosted by the Republican Jewish Coalition. The second party was the one I was really looking forward to the whole week. It was sponsored by *Human Events*, which called itself President

Ronald Reagan's favorite newspaper, and the conservative organization that hosted the largest annual gathering of conservatives——the
one where Joe and I met. It was at a historical building called the
Rotunda and, better yet, I was sure to know people at that one.

After freshening up my makeup, I changed from black pants into a
black skirt while Joe sat at the computer checking e-mail.

"Are you sure we're both on the list for the Rotunda party?" he
asked.

"Yes, I told Stacie we would both be there."

"You're changing again?" he asked.

"Just the bottoms. A skirt looks better with this top."

It was great to visit the Plaza, but the party wasn't that great.

When we arrived at the Rotunda party, there was already a line to
get in. A red carpet covered the dingy New York sidewalk while three
staffers checked people off a list. Just as I stepped up to the table, my
ankle rolled into a hole disguised by the carpet. I went down.

"Are you OK?" the blonde staffer asked.

"Yeah, just my ego is bruised. There's a hole or something under the
carpet," I said.

"Oh, we'll have someone look at that."

Yeah, great, I thought. She crossed my name off the list and I went
in. Since Joe managed to get in without falling on his face, he was
already waiting inside.

"I totally just rolled my ankle on the red carpet," I told him.

"Maybe you should have worn the pants," he said.

"No one saw anything! I just sort of fell on my knees."

"Ann's here."

"Oh, let me go say hi," I said.

It was easy to spot Ann Coulter in a crowd. She was over six feet
tall in heels and surrounded by men. I went over and tapped her on
the arm. She immediately stopped talking to the group of men and
shouted, "Oh, Lisa! It's so great that you're here! You have to meet this
guy. He's the one behind the Swift Boat veterans!"

I shook his hand and, as I am wont to do, awkwardly stood there.

"Also, my parents are here! You have to meet them!"

She grabbed my arm and led me to a small cocktail table in the
middle of the crowded sea of conservatives. "Mother, this is the girl
that wrote those nice book reviews in *Human Events!*"

I shook their hands and said hello.

"It's so crowded in here. They haven't even gotten anything to eat yet!" Ann said.

"Oh, I can go get them a couple of plates," I said.

I was always more comfortable having a purpose at an event. Unlike most people in DC, collecting business cards is never on my to-do list. I went to the buffet and found it already pretty picked over. The prime rib carving station was still open, and there were a few cocktail shrimps. I brought the plates of beef over to her parents and then immediately remembered that they both had heart issues. "I'm sorry, this is all they had!" I told the group.

Eventually I ran into Joe. He had a drink but didn't look that happy.

"I've been talking to people! Aren't you proud of me?" I asked him.

"Good girl. Are you ready to leave?"

"Really? You're ready to go?"

"We've been here for almost two hours. There's no food left. We can watch the evening speeches."

"OK, well, I guess I'll go say bye to Ann."

I looked over and there was a crowd around her. "Never mind, she's busy. Let's just go."

It was our last day in New York. We didn't have convention passes, so I wanted to hit a few stores for souvenirs. Joe, who lived in New York for a short time, was not into this idea, but he went along.

For the past few days we had been enclosed in a Republican bubble. This was evident when the disheveled barista on Houston Street scornfully looked at my "I [heart] GWB" T-shirt and said, "You really like that guy?"

"Yep!" I said cheerfully.

I hit Bloomingdale's, lingering over the shoe and accessories departments and wishing I had the ability to buy more than the plastic little and medium "brown bag" totes modeled after their iconic brown shopping bags. It's never just about money but about my size. Sure, Bloomingdale's had a plus-size department, but there wasn't an item under $100. The message: sure, you can look good, but you'll have to pay. After Bloomingdale's, I went to one of those cheesy souvenir stores and bought a few cheap items that mortified a former New Yorker like Joe.

We went back to the apartment and packed all our stuff. Before we hit the road, we had plans to have dinner with Joe's parents, his brother, and his brother's wife.

Upon arriving at the Italian restaurant, I was greeted by Joe's mother with a big hug. We were seated at one big table. Even though we had disagreements, it was these kinds of moments that made me think everything was OK with me and Joe. I sat across from his sister-in-law, who talked about her job as a teacher and their plans to start having children. As I looked down the table with the red and white checkered tablecloth and plates of Italian food, I felt like I could eventually be a part of this family. It wasn't perfect, but it felt comfortable and real.

We talked about staying a night at Joe's parents' house in New Jersey but instead opted to drive back to Northern Virginia that night. To get us through the trip, Joe brought along the audio version of *America (The Book)* by the *Daily Show* writers. I was asleep before the "Thomas Jefferson had jungle fever" jokes.

We arrived back in Virginia around 3:00 a.m. Joe dropped me off at my mom's house. After lugging my suitcase upstairs, the first thing I did was open my mom and stepdad's bedroom door. I knew Buster would come running out to greet me. And there he was. My best friend. My family.

The morning after we got back, Joe suggested we go to the gym by his house. When I'm at the gym I usually have a plan: cardio, then upper or lower body workout. When possible, I try to use free weights more than machines. Joe didn't seem to have a plan but just sort of wandered around the machines. I teased him when I used the leg press after him and did more than twice the weight with no difficulty. Having grown up a chubby kid who never excelled in anything athletic, I probably enjoyed my new abilities a little too much.

After the gym, we went back to Joe's. He had some errands to run and I still needed to take my stuff and Buster home. Since it was the end of the weekend, it would probably be another week before we saw each other.

"Alright, see you later," Joe said.

"What, no kiss?" I said.

Joe stepped forward and gave me a quick peck. Something was off.

After I was home for a few hours, I decided to call Joe. I was having the uneasy feeling again.

"Hey, it's me," I said.

"Oh, hi."

"Listen, you seemed really off today."

"I'm just tired."

"I just feel like things are weird between us. Like you want to break up."

"But we are broken up," he said.

"What? What do you mean?"

"I told you I wasn't happy when we were driving back from Keswick."

"I didn't know that meant we were breaking up. I wouldn't have gone to New York with you if I thought we were broken up."

"I'm sorry, it's just something I want to do."

"OK."

We hung up. Once again, I was caught off guard. Even the good Catholic boys couldn't be persuaded to stay with me. I instantly thought about when I changed in front of him when we were in New York. When I asked for a kiss earlier today. I felt humiliated. It reminded me of my last day at Chaires Elementary School. I was in fifth grade and changing schools. It was our recess period and my two best friends, Allison and Marianne, and I were sitting on the bleachers.

"Since it's your last day, we really want to ask you something!" Allison said.

"OK, what?" I said.

They both giggled. "You ask her!" Marianne said.

"I will, I will," Allison said.

"Geez, what?" I said.

"OK, why are you so fat?" Allison said.

I pretended to be shocked and then laughed. I can't even remember if I answered the question. Even though I was only ten years old, I knew that I never wanted to let people know how I was really feeling. That was the day I also learned that friends weren't always what they seemed. Sure, they're nice to your face, but once you leave they're laughing behind your back.

Things are never as they seem. Friends aren't always friends. The guy who is nice to you is nice because he's nice. It's not because there's something deeper.

10

Joe tried to stay in touch via e-mail. I despise the "staying friends" concept. If you break up with me, you don't get to be my friend. I responded to e-mails when needed but avoided ever seeing him. Then the big conservative conference came around. I knew he would be there, and avoiding him would be too obvious.

The conference was at the Ronald Reagan Building that year. I was fortunate to be able to introduce one of the conference's most popular speakers and take part in one of the biggest surprises at the conference——a walk-on appearance by Matt Drudge.

Eventually, Joe and I met up at the conference. It was awkward. For me, anyway. I began to wonder if Joe ever thought of me as anything but a friend with benefits. After all, we never said "I love you." It was because he didn't and, therefore, I didn't.

I then found out he was back together with the woman he dated before me. A few months after that I was fired from my job. Once again, blindsided. I had just presided over the institute's most successful lecture program year and got a segment of one of our lectures on *The O'Reilly Factor* the night before. I went back to my office and cried.

During my six months of unemployment, I worked part-time in the same public relations firm as Joe. He was good about not talking about his personal life. I didn't know if it was because of me or because he just didn't talk about it at work. All that I knew came from his boss in offhand comments.

Then there was the day an offhand comment felt like a punch in the stomach.

"Joe probably knows because his fiancée is Jewish," his boss said to me.

Fiancée?

Jewish?

Now I had two more pieces of the puzzle as to why Joe and I broke up. The things I told myself—and others——weren't true. It wasn't because he didn't want to get married. It wasn't because I wasn't Catholic. So, what was left? My looks? My personality? Both?

Around that time, I heard of a job opening for the director of the conservative conference I went to every year. I actually had avoided it that year because I was so embarrassed at not having a job. Since Joe knew the outgoing director who was leaving, I talked to him about applying for the position.

"I don't know if I can do it," I said.

"Sure you can," he said.

"I'm nothing like Stacie."

"That's a good thing."

"I mean I'm not into the networking thing. I can't do it."

"You can do it."

My years spent being a go-between for the last two conference directors paid off. They both put in a good word for me. I got the job.

As noted philosopher Bridget Jones said, "It is a truth universally acknowledged that when one part of your life starts going okay, another falls spectacularly to pieces."

Despite my initial hesitation about applying for the job, I excelled at it. It was my life. Meanwhile, everyone else around me actually had a life. Joe got married on 07-07-07. A year or two after that, he and his wife had a baby. I was sad. It wasn't unrequited love, but an unrequited life.

True to form, I never stayed true to my promise to myself to keep Joe out of my life. For years after we broke up, we were still friends. He filled the logistical void of not having a significant other. I relied on him for lunch when I was busy at work, had a broken appliance, or needed a ride to the airport. Isn't the whole point of being in a relationship so you have a ride to and from the airport?

One afternoon we got together for smoothies. As we waited for them to arrive, I got the nerve to finally ask THE question.

"So, why did you break up with me?" I asked.

"Really?"

"Yes, I never knew why."

"Because I realized I could never make you happy," he said.

The lesson from my relationship with Joe? Don't ask the question if you don't want to hear the answer. I knew Chris had influenced my decision to abandon God. Did he also influence my ability to be happy?

BUSTER

11

I'll never forget the first time I saw him. We met online in 1999 and I fell for him instantly. He had the most beautiful brown eyes. Then he was just known as number 81 by the Washington Humane Society. He was a beagle and chocolate lab mix. The adoption process took a bit of time. When I visited him at his short-term foster home, I sat on the floor and he came right up to me and licked my face. It was true love.

Even though I had only met him once, I fought for him. The woman fostering him didn't seem to want to give him up despite having me go through the process. She even changed his name from Brandon (dumb) to Player (dumber). It was obvious to me that he was a Buster. I think it was more likely that she just didn't care about anyone's schedule but her own. Four days before Christmas I showed up unannounced and took Buster home. He was now my Buster.

Since it was near Christmas, my sister was visiting my mom and stepdad, who lived nearby. They were all waiting in the car when I left Buster's former foster home with Buster following behind me. On the drive back to my mom and stepdad's house, my sister and I sat in the backseat and Buster sat on my lap.

"You're going to have no problem getting a boyfriend now!" my sister said.

Not two seconds later, when we were stopped at a light, a guy in the car next to us looked over at Buster staring out the window and smiled.

"See! I told you!" my sister exclaimed.

It was nice to think about, but even I knew it wouldn't be that easy.

The difference between Chris the Atheist and Joe the Catholic was most pronounced when it came to how they dealt with Buster. Chris was a cat person. But having one view wasn't enough for him. He had to denigrate the opposing view. Chris's cat versus dog views were like his views on religion. It wasn't enough to just accept that some people are religious and some people are not. You had to be an atheist or a true believer. And if you were a true believer, you were ignorant.

Chris talked disdainfully about how when scared, a dog's tail involuntarily covered its genitals. "How can anyone respect an animal that does that?" he said.

My reaction to this was "who cares?" To make his case against dogs, no reason was too small.

Years after we broke up, I'm still haunted thinking about the time I spent away from Buster to spend time with Chris. I frequently would drop him off at my mom's house for a night or two, so he wasn't really alone. I never left him alone overnight by himself. But it was time I'll never get back. I'm also haunted by the fact that I chose to spend time with a person who didn't love me as I was.

Unlike humans, a dog's best quality is that it forgives easily, even when we don't forgive ourselves.

Buster liked Joe. I think Joe also liked Buster. He never complained when Buster slept with us or when he wanted to sit between us on the couch. Joe was a dog person. During most of the time we dated, his dog, Minnie, a German shepherd mix, lived with his ex-girlfriend until he moved to an apartment that allowed dogs.

Unfortunately, Minnie and Buster did not get along. Before Minnie came back to live with Joe, I frequently brought Buster to his apartment. He was well behaved, and I wasn't as guilt-ridden about spending time away from home. When Minnie was able to live with Joe, I was back to dropping Buster off at my mom's house. We didn't date that long after that.

When Buster was three or four years old, the veterinarian discovered he had a heart murmur. She recommended he get an EKG, which would cost more than $500. I put it off for what I thought was several months, but I'm ashamed to admit now that it may have been at least a year. The EKG confirmed the murmur was getting worse. She prescribed a medicine that he would need to take every day. It was a small pill, but not small enough. I could cover it in peanut butter, hide it in a Snausage, or wrap it in a piece of cheese and half the time I would find the pill, clean as a whistle, sitting next to an empty dog dish. Sometimes I would try to feed it to him again with a new disguise, but many times I gave up and vowed to do better the next day.

One of my favorite things about Buster was the way he greeted me when I came home. One day I got home from work and Buster didn't come to the door. I walked around the corner and found him sitting on the daybed in the gym area of my townhouse.

"Hey, silly, what are you doing?" I said to him.

The sound of my voice must have given him the energy he needed, because he jumped off the bed. I put on his collar and leash for a walk to the mailbox. He was walking kind of slow, which I chalked up to maybe just waking up from a nap. I unlocked the mailbox and pulled out a bunch of junk mail. I looked down and Buster was unsteady on his feet and then sort of fell down.

"Little boy, are you still tired?" I asked him.

He just looked up at me with his big brown eyes and wagged his tail.

A few weeks later we were at the vet again. The vet recommended getting an X-ray and another EKG. She called me to the hallway where the X-rays were on the wall.

"He definitely had a cardiac event since the last time we looked at him," she said.

"You mean like a heart attack?"

"Yes, though we don't know the severity of it. We need to keep an eye on it and try some different medications."

My eyes welled up with tears.

After several trials of different medications, the vet recommended I take Buster to a cardiologist. By this time, his belly was filling up with fluid from the extra exertion his heart was going through. I would position pillows for him so he could lay with the front of his body elevated, releasing some of the pressure the fluid put on his lungs.

The cardiologist did an ultrasound on Buster's heart and confirmed the vet's diagnosis.

"Unfortunately, we're looking at end-stage cardiac disease."

I felt like I was kicked in the stomach. End stage? How could this be the end? Buster was barely ten years old. And I had only had him for eight and a half years.

"Is there anything you can do?" I asked, holding back tears while Buster looked at me with his big, brown eyes.

"Well, if he were a human, this is when we would be talking about a heart transplant. At this point, all we can do is make him more comfortable and make sure he isn't subject to any unnecessary exertion. Do you have stairs in your house?"

"Yes, it's a three-story townhouse," I said apologetically.

I wanted to get back to talking about a heart transplant, knowing it wasn't a really possibility.

"He really shouldn't be going up and down stairs. I would carry him as much as you can. I can also drain some of the fluid in his belly in order to make him more comfortable."

"OK," I said.

Before the procedure, I took Buster outside to go to the bathroom. I watched him meander around the small patch of grass. He moved slower, but I never heard him whimper in pain. I decided we could get through this.

We went back inside and they drained the excess fluid, which amounted to nearly four pounds, from Buster's belly. The cardiologist said I should keep an eye on the circumference of his belly to keep track of how quickly the fluid would come back. When he came trotting out of the room, he seemed to have a spring in his step. I saw a glimpse of my old, playful Buster.

A little more than a week later, his belly had already expanded four inches, a lot for his small, nineteen-pound frame. The cardiologist wasn't able to fit him in that day, so I took him to another place. For a fleeting moment, I imagined I could pay the $600 a week for the fluid draining. My credit cards were getting close to their limits; my savings account was dwindling. But every time I handed over my card, I thought it might be the last time. Not because I thought Buster was dying, but because I thought he was sure to get better.

12

My friend Floyd had recently purchased a condo in Palm Beach, Florida. Since I did the invoices for his security business and frequently got him business, I reasoned, and he agreed, that I deserved some time at his condo.

Before embarking on the trip, I wanted to get the OK from the vet. Palm Beach was a sixteen-hour drive from Northern Virginia, so I prepared by mapping out emergency vets every hundred miles from my house to Floyd's condo. If Buster had an emergency, I would never be more than an hour or so from the closest animal hospital. I got copies of his records and X-rays, made sure I had enough medicine, and bought a doggy stroller so he wouldn't have to exert himself in the Florida heat. The vet said he was OK to go but to keep him out of the sun and make sure he got plenty of water.

Buster and I got to Florida with no problems. My friend's condo was on the twelfth floor, so we had to establish a schedule. Buster was taking several diuretics a day to help with the fluid retention. Several times a day I put him in his stroller, took the elevator down, and wheeled him to a nearby grassy area. Even though he was used to being alone when I was at work, I felt guilty leaving him alone in a new place. The only time I ever left the condo in the two weeks I was there was for an hour or two at the pool or to run a quick errand to the grocery store.

When we got back from Florida, it was late August 2008 and most of the conservative movement was in Minneapolis for the Republican National Convention. Most of the people at my work were going, so

I decided to take a few days off and hang out at my friend Simon's house in the suburbs of Maryland. His mother, a special assistant to a prominent lobbyist, and his father, a political reporter, were both at the convention.

Truth be told, I'd had a crush on Simon for many years. He was a musician who lived in his parents' basement. Though he liked to pretend he was living the life of a starving musician, he still pulled in a decent salary, judging by what he was paid for the one week of work during the conservative conference I directed. You had to admire someone who could pull off washing down Brie and Carr's water crackers with Jack Daniels.

By this time I had gained back all the weight I had lost with Chris, plus a lot more. I was never under any illusion that Simon might be attracted to me.

After watching speeches, drinking, and eating pizza, we called it a night. Buster and I went to the guest bedroom upstairs and Simon slept on the couch in the basement. The guest room was so hot. Buster wasn't able to get comfortable and fall asleep; therefore I wasn't able to sleep either. Around 1:00 a.m., I thought it might be better to just drive home. But I didn't want to miss out on the time I was spending with Simon.

I think Buster and I may have eventually fallen asleep, but we were up by six. I showered and we went downstairs, where it was noticeably cooler. A few hours later Simon came up from the basement.

"Wow, it's really hot up here."

"You should go upstairs. It's a sauna."

"It's freezing in the basement."

As it turned out, the air conditioner had frozen over and stopped working. We decided to put Buster in the basement where it was a lot cooler and go bowling. When we got back, the guy who cleaned their house was just leaving.

"Hey, tell your mom that I didn't get to the second floor. It's 110 degrees up there," he said.

It was time to go home.

13

Buster wasn't getting better. The vets were always honest about his condition, but I still held out hope. I hated going to work. Not only did I not want to leave him alone, but I was afraid something might happen to him while I was gone. The thought of him being scared and dying alone was too much to bear.

After a particularly bad weekend, I called in to work on Monday and told a coworker I wouldn't be coming in because Buster was really sick. Then I called the vet. When I spoke to her, I said I might have to bring him in because he was at the end.

I didn't bring him in that day. Instead I spent the day with him, doing nothing. Around 6:00 p.m., I decided to order a special meal for him. We got in the car and I drove to the nearby Chili's to pick up his steak dinner.

When we got home, I rinsed off the spices on the steak and cut it into bite-size pieces. Buster hadn't been eating much of his food lately, but I often thought it was because it was laced with so much medicine that it didn't taste any good. That night I fed him the steak bite by bite.

After another bad night, I woke up and decided we needed to go to the vet. Before we left, I put a few pieces of Pup-Peroni in my pocket. I knew it was going to be a tough trip.

The vet came in and I told her about the last few weeks.

"I think it might be time for him to not be in pain anymore," I said. "He's lived a good life and you've been a good a nurse to him."

I didn't want to hear it. I wanted her to give me options. I wanted her to tell me it wasn't time yet. She left the room to get a tech to help.

I looked into Buster's eyes and pleaded with him to give me a sign.

I offered him a piece of Pup-Peroni and he gently took it out of my fingers and ate it.

The next thing I knew, the tech came in and took Buster to another room to prepare him. Another tech came in with paperwork for me to sign giving the OK to end his life. I was crying so hard, but I signed my name. I kept waiting for someone to tell me that I didn't have to do this, that there were other medicines I could give him or an operation he could have.

Then the tech and the vet came back in with Buster. He was wrapped in a blanket and had an IV in his leg. The tech placed him on the table and the vet administered the drug to put him to sleep. Because he was lying on his side, it was already hard for him to breathe. He was panting, then his breathing started to slow down. Then he was gone. His eyes were still open, but he was gone. The vet and tech left me alone. I sat there, crying, petting his ear and the top of his head. I lost track of how long Buster and I were alone. Eventually, I put on my sunglasses and walked out of the building.

I cried so hard as I drove home that I had to pull over for a few minutes because I couldn't see to drive. When I finally got home, I threw myself on the daybed in the basement. There was a pile of mail on the bed. I picked it up and threw it across the room. Magazines, bills, and junk mail went flying.

I went upstairs. I had done nothing to prepare for the fact that I wouldn't be coming home with Buster. His basket of toys remained in the corner. The pillows were still arranged on the couch for his comfort. His water dish was filled.

I thought about the song I would sing to Buster when he was sick.

You are my sunshine,
My only sunshine.
You make me happy
When skies are grey.
You'll never know, dear,
How much I love you.
Please don't take my sunshine away.

I felt completely empty. He was taken away. "Why?" I cried out to the empty house. At that moment, I knew I was no longer an atheist. I was too angry at God.

JOHN
the Evangelical

14

After nearly three years as director of the largest conservative conference, I was finally starting to feel more comfortable in the position. I had moved from a shared office space to my own office and had a full-time assistant named Thomas. Simon once described Thomas as a boy trapped in a man's body. He was from the Midwest, nerdy, six foot four, and handsome. He was like the son or little brother I never had. He was also well versed in the drama I created in my head between me and Simon. We joked about it, never admitting out loud that I found it virtually implausible that any guy would be attracted to me. Having a crush on an unattainable person (even an unemployed musician who lived in his parents' basement) hid the fact that I did not date by circumstance rather than by choice.

Work was my life. And watching reality TV. Talking on the phone with relatives was always a race to say good-bye before the "So, are you dating anyone?" question.

As the conference approached, I watched less TV. It was January 2009, just a few weeks before the conference. Thomas and I were now working twelve to fourteen hours a day, including on weekends. In addition to the logistical details that came with planning a conference of more than eight thousand people, I had to deal with all the people who thought they deserved a speaking slot. Also, I hadn't released the schedule yet, so everyone was asking about it.

Early in the day, I got an e-mail from a guy I didn't even know regarding the schedule.

Lisa!

When you have a chance, please send me the schedule. Happy to help fill in some holes.

John

Who did this guy think he was? During my daily phone call with Simon, I relayed the random e-mail to him.

"Oh, no, he's good people. Send him what he wants," he said.

"Well, first I have to ask the chairman."

"He'll say it's fine," Simon said.

And he did. In fact, he also said it was OK to move on whatever suggestions John had for the schedule. Again, I wondered, who was this guy?

Once the schedule was released a few days later, the calls from people who thought they should be on a particular panel, in a particular room, or on a particular day dominated my e-mail and voicemail. One guy was a particular pain in the ass. He left multiple messages and sent multiple e-mails to me and the chairman insisting that he be on the Hollywood panel because he had made a political documentary. He was approaching conspiracy theory–level paranoia on why he wasn't included. I knew I could only avoid his phone calls for so long.

Then came an e-mail from the infamous John.

Conference Queen,

Not to worry. The so-called filmmaker will not be bothering you. He has been told to stand down and take the speaking slot he's been given.

Your Intern

I was stunned. I fired off a response.

John,

You're like Batman! Thank you so much for making this problem child go away.

I am forever in your debt.

Conference Princess (I like to think I'm not old enough to be a queen yet)

From then on, I always called him Batman.

The conference was in full swing. It was the last day, but it was the most nerve-wracking for me because I would soon be introducing the closing speaker and my political hero, Rush Limbaugh. I was running back and forth between my on-site office, backstage, and the green room. As I was about to reach for the door, it flew open. There stood a tall man who was balding but still had some curly brown hair. I knew I had seen him before—one of those guys who seemed to always be around the important people but didn't demand it. His height put his name badge right at my eye level. John.

"Batman!" I exclaimed.

"Hey!"

I immediately got the feeling that he had recognized me before I recognized him. I suppose after a few years of being backstage, I was probably one of the familiar faces compared to the ever-changing cast of speakers and organization members.

"I'm so glad I finally ran into you on the last day!" I said.

"Are you ready for your big intro?"

"No! I haven't even written it yet. I know the story I want to tell, but I haven't written anything down. I have a few minutes now, so I'm going to lock myself in the VIP room. Do you want to help me?"

"Sure, I have a few minutes," he said after checking his watch.

I led him to the VIP room, where Rush and only a few select speakers were allowed.

"I didn't even know this was back here," he said.

"Really? You didn't come back here with your guy?"

"No, we went directly backstage."

"Well, now you know. Of course, when Rush gets here, no one will be allowed back here. Not even Batman."

"Ha! Don't worry. I'll keep a safe distance. So, what's the story you want to tell?" he asked.

"I want to talk about this guy I had a crush on in high school. We were like the only conservatives in class. At least the only ones that enjoyed fighting with the teacher. One day he asked if I ever listened to Rush Limbaugh. I said I didn't. Then he told me he listened to it in his car during the lunch break and that I should come out and listen with him some time."

"That is priceless! You have to tell that story."

"But it could get a little risqué. Not because anything risqué happened—I was a chubby good girl——but because that's what makes the story funny."

"OK, what's your line?"

"I love that you know I already have a line!" I said. "OK, here it is: I became a conservative in the backseat of a Nissan 300zx"

"That's great! You'll have the crowd roaring!" he said.

"OK, but I was thinking of changing the car to a Camaro. Also, we were obviously in the front seat, but I think saying backseat of a Camaro is funnier."

"It is. You've crafted a perfect line. Is David going to be on the stage, too?" he said, referring to the chairman of my conference.

"Yep, he'll be up there because they'll have just finished announcing the straw poll results."

"You need a good line for him, too."

"OK, but I want the entire intro to be under sixty seconds. Everyone will just be waiting for me to get off the stage," I said.

"I know, I know, but you need a line acknowledging that he's the godfather of the conservative family reunion. Just say that."

"Now I need to type this up. Will I see you later?"

"Of course! I'll be backstage cheering you on."

A few hours later I walked on stage. The energy in the ballroom was unbelievable. So much was going on that I couldn't even process what was about to happen. Here I was introducing the biggest name in conservative politics in a speech that was being broadcast live by Fox News, CNN, and C-SPAN and covered by hundreds of reporters in a room of a thousand people and overflow rooms with more thousands of people.

I delivered my laugh line and, like a pro, didn't talk over the laughter. I finished and the Pretenders "My City Was Gone" played over the sound system. The crowd went wild. They were on their feet and cheering loudly. Even though we had previously talked and took pictures in the VIP room when he arrived, Rush hugged me and kissed me on the cheek when he got to the podium. He then went into what has now become an iconic speech, sporadically fist-bumping me and the chairman.

After the conference ended, we had a party for the volunteers and staff in the presidential suite. For the last two years I had avoided the party. I later found out that many of the volunteers viewed me as a snob. In reality, it was just my usual discomfort around large groups of people.

When I walked into the suite, everyone cheered and fist-bumped me like Rush had done. The attention caught me by surprise. It was humbling to see all these people who worked to make the conference, and me by extension, look good.

I saw Simon over by the bar and walked over.

"Can you believe this is my first volunteer party?" I said.

Simon grabbed me by the shoulders and kissed me on the mouth.

"I'm so proud of you," he said.

I knew the kiss meant nothing. We were all on a post-conference high. I talked to several volunteers, many for the first time. They were all so excited to have been part of an event at the center of our political universe.

Then a scene shocked me back to reality. In the corner, Simon was talking to an awkwardly pretty volunteer. She was wearing a purple dress, one of those kinds that are tight on the thighs but blousy on the top. Basically, you can't have a hint of a stomach in order to wear it. I could tell she was smitten. I was quickly reminded that despite the success of the last three days, there were still some things I would never have and never be. I had to get out of there.

Without saying good-bye, I tried to get to the door as fast as possible. Just as the door was about to close, my assistant, Thomas, caught it.

"Lisa, where are you going?" he asked.

"Back to my room. I'm tired."

"Why? Everyone wants you to stay. This is your moment."

"Please, no one cares. It's just the end of the conference and people want to drink," I said.

"I want you to stay."

"I'm tired and just want to go back to my room."

"OK. Can I at least have a hug? We have another year behind us!"

This was our third conference together. I turned back, gave him a quick hug, and, without a word, walked away. Being cold was my way of hiding that I didn't even have the self-confidence to be in a room full of people singing my praises. At this moment there was only one thought on my mind: I was fatter than everyone in the room.

For the next month or so, the political media continued to revolve around Rush's closing speech. There were photos and TV clips. The folks on the left talked about Rush's weight. And I was, once again, reminded of how much weight I had gained. I read a comment in one article from someone remarking he was surprised the stage didn't collapse under the weight of the two of us. After reading that, I avoided any other comments.

A few weeks later, Rush announced on his radio show that he was starting a weight-loss regimen and was already down several pounds. A few months later, he had lost eighty pounds. I was still the same, perhaps even a few pounds heavier. I decided to make a permanent change.

The previous summer when I was in Palm Beach, a friend told me about her friend who had undergone Lap-Band surgery. Supposedly, it was less invasive than gastric bypass and, more importantly, was adjustable.

The Lap-Band procedure appealed to me because it removed a lot of the decision making. From what I read, most people who'd had it found it difficult to eat foods like bread, pasta, and rice—basically, anything that could expand after you eat it and cause trouble for the band. The hard-line restrictions gave me comfort.

As with any surgery, there were risks. I didn't care. At that point in my life, I didn't care what happened to my body. I also worried that because someone I really respected came to me with the idea, I would be letting her down if I didn't do it. I Googled "lap band doctors," found one near me, and made an appointment for a consultation.

I intended to get the surgery as soon as possible. Since the annual conference had just finished, I had plenty of time to get through the slew of mandatory appointments and exams. I went from never going to the doctor to having two or three appointments a week.

One of the requirements for insurance coverage was passing a psychological test. It was over four hundred questions, many of them repeats or the same question asked in a different way to ensure you weren't faking the answers, I suppose. Several questions asked about my religious beliefs . . .

"I gain strength from a creator."

"God has a plan for me."

Definitely Agree, Mostly Agree, Somewhat Agree, or Don't Agree At All?

Don't agree at all.

When the results came back, I had to sit with a psychologist and go over her findings.

"You gravitate toward black and white thinking. You see things as right or wrong," she said.

"OK."

"And then on your spiritual side, you scored very low, which just means you don't turn to a religious being for guidance," she said.

I took that as a compliment. My test showed that I saw the world in absolutes and I didn't need a bearded man in the sky to tell me what was right and wrong.

I decided not to tell very many people about the surgery. Despite the message I was getting from discussion boards and consultations with the doctors that this was just a tool to weight loss and not an easy fix, I was embarrassed about it. I didn't want to deal with people's expectations of quick weight loss for me or judgment about taking the easy way out. Of course, these thoughts were also my own.

Given that my eating habits were about to change drastically, it became clear that I wouldn't be able to get away with saying "I'm not hungry" with people who spent a lot of time with me. A part of me also thought it was the final hand I could play with Simon. Maybe if he knew I was going to be losing weight, things would be different between us.

A few weeks later, we were at a bar across the street from the conference venue. We had just wrapped up a few final shipments. That year's conference was now officially over. Thomas got up to go to the bathroom and it was just me and Simon.

"I have to tell you something I'm doing. It's already set, so I don't really want to have a discussion about it," I said.

"OK."

"In a few weeks I'm getting Lap-Band surgery."

"OK."

"It's time I got serious about my life. Some friends suggested it."

"Is that why you're doing it?"

"No, I'm doing it because I want to. I just heard about it through them."

"Well, I'm proud of you then."

Just then Thomas came back from the bathroom. I immediately felt guilty for not telling him. Thomas and I spent every workday together. We weren't just coworkers, but friends.

"What's going on?" Thomas said.

"I was just telling Simon that I'm having surgery soon."

"What? What surgery?"

"I'm having Lap-Band surgery. It's where they put a band over the top of your stomach so you eat less. It also limits the foods you can actually eat. So, no more rice, bread, or pasta and a lot less of everything else."

Thomas looked down and there was quiet for a few seconds. I wondered what he was thinking.

"Is that what you want to do?" he finally said.

"Yep, the surgery is in a few weeks."

"Then I think that's really cool."

Several weeks later, I got a rare e-mail from Simon.

I had a dream about you. Post-op. You looked good. And happy. Had
that wicked-ass up-to-no good smirk on your face.

By the time my surgery date had come around, I had told a handful of people. I broke down and told my mom, dad, and sister. Since I was going in for major surgery, I decided it might be good for someone I was actually related to should know that I was in the hospital.

Thomas dropped me off at the hospital early on Friday morning. I checked myself in, then waited. I'd never had surgery and really didn't know what to expect.

"Are you ready to get going?"

My head jerked up. "Oh, yeah, it beats waiting," I said to the nurse.

"Great. Well, here's a bag for your stuff. Is there anyone here with you today?" he said.

"No, just me."

"OK, you need to take off everything, including everything," he said.

"Well, that's easy enough to remember."

"Yep, I figure that's the best way to get around all the list of stuff people ask."

Within an hour, I was in the bed, hooked up to an IV, and waiting to be wheeled into surgery.

"It's your turn, Lisa," said another nurse.

Then me and my bed were on the move. When I arrived in the oper-
ating room, I was surprised at how bright it was. There were lots of
people making preparations. It started to get overwhelming. My arms
were strapped as if I were on a cross. It reminded me of when I signed
the papers to have Buster put to sleep. Everyone was moving too fast.
My brain hadn't caught up yet. Wasn't there still time to turn back?
Then the anesthesia kicked in and I was out.

I didn't dream. It was like I was in nothingness. I woke up to the
nurses calling my name.

"Lisa, you're done. Stay awake now."

My eyes were still heavy. I wanted to drift back to sleep.

"Lisa! Lisa! Wake up. You can't go to your room until you stay
awake."

Eventually I was wheeled to my own room. Moving from bed to
bed wasn't as difficult as I thought. Once I got settled, I looked around
the room and realized I was alone. No flowers, no family to greet me
once I was out of surgery. It was just me in my bed. My thoughts were
soon quieted when a nurse came and explained that the morphine drip
was now on and that nurses would be coming in periodically to check
bandages. If I needed to go to the bathroom, I was to ring the nurses'
station so they could undo the circulators around my legs. She also
said I should try to walk as much as I could.

The constant liquid intake from the IV made ringing the nurses' station a frequent occurrence. I managed a few hours of sleep. The single
greatest moment was finally getting ice chips after nearly twenty-four
hours without water or food.

Oddly, I was kind of sad about leaving the hospital the next morning.
It was nice not having to make any decisions. The drugs weren't bad
either.

Around noon, Thomas picked me up. I was home within an hour.
I was disappointed to find that I had gained nine pounds while in the
hospital. Stupid IV drip.

15

It had been nearly six months since my surgery and I had lost almost fifty pounds. I was used to eating in a new way——small portions, small bites, a lot of chewing, but still having trouble every once in a while. It was known on the Lap-Band discussion threads as a "productive burp." For me, it was just throwing up.

I was in Florida to visit my dad for his birthday, which was just before a small gathering of neoconservatives was taking place in Palm Beach. It was held at the Breakers resort. I was looking forward to getting away for a weekend before the craziness of the next conference. I was also nervous about seeing people because I knew their expectations might be that weight-loss surgery meant "you should be skinny by now." My dad must have called me five times asking what I could eat. I kept telling him that I didn't eat much, so there was no need to buy anything special. The last thing I wanted to do was call attention to my eating habits.

After a few days in Tallahassee, I got a rental car and made my way down to Palm Beach. As I was checking into the Breakers, my phone rang. I didn't recognize the number and check-in was taking longer than expected, so I answered it.

"This is Lisa," I said.

"Breakers Babe! It's John."

"Batman! How did you know I'm at the Breakers? I'm just checking in now."

"I'm here, too. I just saw your name on the attendee list. Just when I thought no one cool was going to be here, I saw your name."

"Oh, yay! Floyd and his girlfriend, Colleen, are also here. I haven't met her yet," I said.

"This is going to be fun. You finish getting checked in and I'll see you at the reception tonight."

I dropped my bags off in my room. Sadly, it was another year at the Breakers without an ocean-view room. Two years priors I had attended this event and spent most of my time in my hotel room. It was another instance of being overwhelmed by the feeling of being alone and like I didn't belong. I felt like I was perpetually in that moment in *Dirty Dancing* when Johnny teaches Baby to dirty dance. When it ends, she thought they were having a moment, but she soon found herself dancing alone and looking like a fool.

From the outside, people might have thought I did this to draw attention to myself. To get attention and have people beg me to come out. That truly was not the case. The more people pleaded, the more I withdrew.

This year I was excited that it might be different. I returned the rental car to the airport and then took a town car back to the hotel to freshen up. Despite having lost over fifty pounds, I still wore a lot of the same clothes. I wasn't sure how dressy the reception would be that year, so I opted for black leggings and a zebra-print tunic with yellow stones along the collar.

Floyd, the bodyguard for nearly every important conservative event and one of my best friends, was standing at the entrance of the courtyard. I tapped him on the shoulder.

"Boop" he said, using his nickname for me. "I was wondering where you were. You look great!" he said.

"Where's Colleen?" I asked.

"She's still upstairs getting ready. I told her I had to come down before everyone else, so she would have to come down on her own if she wasn't ready."

"Guess who is also going to be here? John!"

"Who?" he said.

"You know, the guy from the conference who was backstage all the time."

"There were a lot of people backstage."

"Trust me, you'll know him when you see him."

And as if on cue, John was coming up the stairs.

"Batman, meet Superman!" I said.

"Huh? Oh yeah, hey man," Floyd said.

"Neither one of you have a drink! What do you want?" John said.

John always seemed to operate on eleven, as the boys from Spinal Tap would say. Within in minutes he was back with a drink for me and himself. Floyd was still on duty, so he had to decline. John and I walked over to a highboy cocktail table in the courtyard.

As we made small talk about the conference and who was there, Betsy, a woman I frequently used as an emcee during the conference, joined us. She was also the president of a prominent publishing house. Within a few minutes, we were talking about dating.

"Is your new husband here?" John asked.

"Oh! I didn't know you got married. Congratulations!" I said.

"Thank you! Yes, we've been married a few months It's been great," Betsy said.

"How did you meet?" I asked.

"On Match.com, actually. I know, I know. We had a great first date though," she said.

"When did you know it was serious?" I asked.

"Probably on the first date."

"OK, what did he do to put him over the top?" John asked.

"Well, over the course of exchanging e-mails and phone calls, we talked about wine and I mentioned my favorite. For our first date, he called a bunch of restaurants and found one that had it and made sure it was there waiting when we arrived," Betsy said.

"Aww! That is so sweet. You found a good one," I said.

"Yes, I did," she said.

"I'm over all the guys in DC," I said. "Most of them are just looking for a second income."

"See, that's not me. If my wife wanted to have a career, that's fine. If she wants to stay home and keep the cupboard warm, that's fine, too," John said.

At that moment, I looked at him in a new light. He was tall, at least six foot four. He had brown, curly hair. He had a good smile. A fantastic smile, actually. It seemed to take over every muscle in his face, giving him those lines around his eyes that make guys look distinguished and women look old. I willed Betsy to ask John the question I didn't want to ask.

"Are you dating anyone now?" she obliged.

Thank you, Betsy!

"No, I can't subject a woman to my crazy travel schedule right now. I travel too much. I mean, if there was a woman who wanted to travel with me that would be great, but I could never ask someone to do that," John said.

"Well, that's good that you know that about yourself. And on that note, I need to get back to my room and call my hubby and kids before they all hit the feathers," Betsy said.

We said our good-byes. The reception was starting to wrap up.

"I think Floyd is meeting his girlfriend at the bar if you want to grab a drink there," I said.

"Yes! And I need something to eat. I haven't eaten all day," John said.

We made our way to the ocean-themed restaurant at the Breakers and grabbed a corner table.

"So, tell me all the conference gossip!" John said.

No joke, the man talks in exclamation points. I found myself matching his enthusiasm.

"Oh, it's too early for any real drama! You probably have more dirt than I do at this point, Batman."

"OK, then let's order and then tell me what's going on with you. Do you eat nachos?"

"Yep, I can eat them, but order whatever you want because I won't each much."

"Nachos and one more round of drinks it is. I like this plan."

After having surgery, there was nothing I dreaded more than the ordering process. One of the benefits of the gastric band versus the bypass is that it's adjustable so you can (mostly) eat real food. Which means one of the drawbacks is also that you can eat real food. The waitress eventually came to the table.

"We're ready! Bombay on the rocks for me, Crown and ginger ale for the lady, and the nachos without onions. Save them for the starving children," John said.

The waitress smirked and walked away. Apparently, John's charms only worked on me. I could live with that.

"OK, what's going on with you? How's the job? How's your life?"

"Everything's going along. I'm still getting used to life after the surgery. Weight loss isn't as fast as I thought it would be."

That was my armor——reminding people it was a slow process so they wouldn't judge my progress too harshly. When people get weight-loss surgery, their friends and family often expect the weight to fly off. Even now, I have friends who ask every week how much weight I've lost. The reality is that some weeks the numbers don't change, and I feel like I've disappointed them more than I've disappointed myself.

"You look great. I noticed right away," said John.

"I've lost about fifty pounds so far, but I still have a long way to go," I said.

This was another frequent disclaimer. It was my way of telling people I wasn't blind to the fact that I had a lot more to lose.

We talked about presidential politics. As usual, John had all the answers. Then the conversation turned to the future.

"What do you want to do?" he asked.

"Well, I've always wanted to be a stay-at-home mom, but I think my time has passed for that."

"Oh, that's ridiculous."

"No, it's not. It's biology, Batman."

"No, it's ridiculous because you need to have faith that there are a million other options for your life."

"Yeah, faith is my problem."

"What do you mean?" he asked.

"I've tried to have a connection to God, but I just feel like I've been so negative against him for so long that my heart is totally closed to it. Like being a Christian is a club I can't join."

I don't know if I had one too many drinks or if it was the enormity of what I'd just admitted——that I wasn't good enough for God—— but tears sprang to my eyes. John placed his hand on mine.

"God wants you in his life," he said. "The club is open to everyone."

"I know, I know. I'm just saying I don't think my heart will ever be open to it."

"You'll get there. You can always ask me anything if you have questions."

After finishing our drinks and nachos, John walked me to my hotel room. We talked for a bit in the doorway, he hugged me, and then we said our good-byes until the conference the next morning. I was starting to feel something. And it wasn't the Holy Spirit.

The next morning I was giddy at the prospect of spending more time with John. At the first session he sat down next to me. With our legal pads and the classroom-style seating, I felt like we were in school. I was already knee-deep in a schoolgirl crush. During the first panel, a well-known writer and magazine editor was at the podium. Having heard him speak at several events and even participated in a panel with him, I knew what to expect.

"I'll make a bet with you," I whispered.

"OK, what's the bet?"

"I'll bet you five bucks that Jonah makes a *Simpsons* reference in his talk on Israel."

"Ha! You're on."

John took a five-dollar bill out of his wallet and placed it on the table. I did the same.

Jonah talked for nearly twenty minutes. Then, I heard it as clear as day.

"We're talking about a foreign policy that Bart Simpson would do . . ."

I had to sit on my hands and bite my tongue to keep from making a scene. John and I immediately looked at one another. My eyes were wide and expectant. He smiled and said, "You win!"

I was ecstatic. My $5 bet felt like $5 million.

After a day of sessions, there was a break for the afternoon to enjoy the resort. Floyd's girlfriend made appointments for us at the spa for a manicure and pedicure, but beyond that I didn't have anything planned.

After our spa session, I texted John to see what was going on. I didn't get an immediate response, so I went back to my room. Hotel rooms were always my safe space. I could hide out and if I didn't answer a phone call or text, people usually assumed I was busy enjoying (in this case) the four-star resort, not watching the movie preview channel with the drapes closed.

My phone buzzed. It was John. "Come to the pool bar! With Pat C.!"

I surveyed myself in the mirror. I was overdressed for the pool bar, but I was wearing a flattering outfit. My white pants were new and tight enough to give me a waist, unlike many of the other pants I was still holding on to. My top was Pucci inspired (I was still way above actual Pucci size), with a keyhole neckline and empire waist that cinched in the back. I decided it was worth it to stay more dressed up.

As I neared the pool, I saw the head of an organization that made conservative documentaries. He was playing with his kids in the pool. At the exact moment I was passing the pool, he was getting out. Hairy belly in full view and dripping wet, he said, "Hey there."

"Hi, how are you?"

"Oh you know, chasing kids."

I smiled and kept walking. Yeah, I was OK with staying overdressed.

I looked around the bar and saw John sitting with Pat and four other people around a small table. I decided to play dumb and grab a small table out of the way. It gave me the ability to say I was there but also avoid the awkwardness of walking up to a group of people. Thankfully, I brought pen and paper and could pretend to work while sipping an overly priced, overly fruity drink. It takes a lot of work to pull off the relaxed look.

Out of the corner of my eye, I saw John get up from his table and go inside. After a few minutes, he came out and noticed me at my table.

"What are you doing here? We have a table over there!"

"Oh, I didn't see you," I lied. "I just thought you had left by the time I got here."

"No, we've been here all afternoon. Come join us!"

"No, I'm just finishing up and need to go back to my room before dinner. Are you going to the dinner?"

"Of course. I'll get us the best table."

"OK, see you in a few!" I said.

John walked away and I took in his attire. He was wearing a yellow polo shirt, white shorts, and a baseball hat. He looked considerably younger and more fit than I thought. I was already mentally peeling back the age difference. If I was an old thirty-three and he a young forty-eight, we were not far apart at all.

For dinner, I decided to wear the white pants again but change tops. One of the benefits of weight loss was that even though my breasts were slightly smaller, they seemed larger in comparison to the rest of me. And a girl needs to know her best assets (eyes, boobs, hair, in that order). I wore an embellished hot-pink blouse with a deep plunging V-neck. Of course, I immediately regretted my choice when Floyd, as a big brother would, made a comment.

"Whoa, Boop!" Floyd said. "Your boobs are enormous."

"Floyd, shut up!"

Even though the intention was to draw attention to them, my breasts also conjured up insecurities. My sister and mother, both thin, were not well endowed. I recalled my sister once saying with disdain, "Boobs are just fat."

"Where's Colleen?" I asked.

"She's on her way down. After listening to her say 'five more minutes' for the last hour, I told her I had to go down without her. I'm here to work."

"Well, make sure she sits at our table. John said he was saving a cool people table."

"Yeah, you'll see her when she comes down. She doesn't know anyone here. This isn't her thing. She'll definitely want to sit with you."

"OK. I think I like John."

"Really? Boop, are you trying to get some action this weekend?"

I punched him in the arm. "Floyd, stop it."

"That explains the blouse."

"Now you're embarrassing me, so I'm walking away."

I hated that Floyd or anyone thought I was trying. Accidentally showing cleavage was sexy. Trying——and failing——to be sexy was sad. I saw John at a table toward the back.

"Welcome to the cool kids' table!" he said.

"Who are the other cool kids?"

"Colleen, of course, my friend Eric Metaxas, Ann, anyone else we see. Grab a seat."

I took a seat facing the stage. As the table began filling up, I became more and more self-conscious. I didn't want to call attention to the fact that I wouldn't be eating much food. Would people really buy that the fat girl wasn't hungry? Perhaps more importantly, why did I care what a bunch of strangers thought?

My self-deprecating train of thought was interrupted by a man standing next to me.

"Is this John's table? I was told to park it here," he said.

"Please do," I said.

We did the political world exchange——name, job, city. He was a writer. When he told me the title of his latest book, it rang a bell.

"Aren't you friends with Ann?" I said.

"Yes, she's a good friend," Eric said.

"What a coincidence! I've been asking her some religious questions lately and she suggested I read your books."

"I'm humbled she would recommend my books. What sort of questions do you have?"

"Well, I guess I'm not really a believer, but I want to be. I'm just afraid it will never click."

"Has Ann told you anything about my conversion?"

"Nope," I said.

"OK, I'll give you the short version. All my life, a lot of ideas and big moments have come to me in dreams. When God showed himself to me, it was in a dream. I don't think I would have been receptive to it any other way."

"That's really interesting. I've been trying to read stuff, listen to stuff. Ann told me to listen to a sermon from the church she goes to in New York."

"Tim Keller?"

"Yep, him."

"What did you think of it?"

"It was good, but I think my hopes were too high."

"What do you mean?" he asked.

"Well, I was hoping because she said this sermon reminded her of me that it would really speak to me. It didn't, though. It was just a good speech."

"For people like you and me, it has to be a big moment. You'll have a conversion moment. A moment when God will show himself to you."

"Well, I hope so. We'll see."

"Do you have any of my books?" he asked.

"Um, no, not yet."

"I just realized I have one book left. I brought a couple with me and have one left. I think this book was meant for you."

"Oh, OK."

"I'll go back to my room and get it," he said as he got up from the table.

Colleen, who was sitting on the other side of me, said, "What's his story?" after he left.

Colleen was great and totally perfect for Floyd. She was petite, but tough. She was a smart aleck, but very sweet.

"Oh, he's a writer who is friends with Ann. It's so funny that he's sitting next to me because she's been telling me to read his books for years," I told her.

"Oh, that is neat."

"What did you end up doing today?" I asked.

"Oh, not much. Went to the gym, walked around for a bit."

"You should come to some of the sessions. Actually, Eric is speaking tomorrow."

"Politics isn't really my thing, but I might come to a few."

"I wonder what they're serving for dinner."

"You didn't eat any of your salad."

"I know, sometimes raw vegetables don't work for me. Also, I can really only eat one course, if that much. Oh, it looks like the entrée is red meat," I said.

"You don't eat red meat?"

"I do, it's just harder to eat."

"Just ask for something else. I'm sure they can give you a fish dish."

"No, it's OK."

"Don't be silly. I'll ask for you."

The last thing I wanted was for what I eat to become a topic of conversation. So, I let Colleen ask. The waiter said it was no problem and soon brought me a lovely piece of halibut. I ate three or four bites.

After dinner, I found Floyd.

"How's it going, Boop?" he said

"One of tomorrow's speakers sat next to me and gave me his book."

I showed him the book and he rolled his eyes.

"I know, I know. It's about religion. Whatever. I'll at least read it just because he's a nice guy," I said.

"So what's the plan?"

"John mentioned getting drinks at the bar afterwards."

"OK, I'll get a drink. But it's been a long day. I don't want to stay up late, and Colleen has been up since 6:00 a.m."

"What? You think I want to party?" I said, laughing.

When Colleen, Floyd, and I got to the bar just down the hall from the banquet room, John already had a table. Sitting with him was Joy, the event planner hired by the organization. I was already familiar with her work.

Colleen whispered to me, "She seems pretty chummy with John."

I looked over and noticed John was holding her hand. Then I looked at her other hand. Yep, she was still married.

"Last year my boss caught her making out with a senator who was a speaker. And she has, like, two kids," I told Colleen.

"What a hussy," she said.

"I know. And she looks old, but I guess John doesn't seem to mind."

She was older (admittedly, probably John's age), had blonde hair with obvious roots, wore a cheap dress that was cut too young for her. And she was completely flat chested. We looked completely different.

As drinks were finishing up, Floyd and Colleen made their move to leave and go back to their room. John announced that we should all go for a walk on the beach in the moonlight.

"Sure," I said.

"Let's go," said Joy.

As we walked on the sidewalk toward the beach, I was behind John and Joy. They were laughing and holding hands. How did I become the third wheel with this guy and a married woman?

"Actually, I'm pretty tired and I'm going to head back to my room," I announced to their backs.

"Oh, don't go! It's a beautiful night!" John said.

"No, I'm just tired. I want to go to bed," I said.

He put his hand on my shoulder and squeezed. "OK, I'll see you tomorrow then?"

"Yep, good night."

I turned and walked as fast and nonchalantly as I could. Just before I opened the door to go back inside the hotel, I heard their carefree laughter. It was now a race to get to my room before tears started falling. It wasn't about John. It was about never being the girl who got the guy. When faced with a choice, he——whoever he was——always chose the other girl. Or in this case, a married woman.

By the next morning, I was still in a sour mood after last night's events. I felt out of place and lonely. Rather than go to breakfast, I opened the minibar, grabbed an $8 Diet Coke, and didn't blink an eye.

As I settled back into bed, a text came from John.

"When are you coming down?"

I texted back: "Laying low today."

He texted back: "But I'm leaving after lunch! Can I come by your room and say goodbye?"

"Sure. 302."

Oh, what to wear to a pity party? I kept my pajamas on, adding a bra and cardigan. Then, I made an attempt at minimal hair and makeup, all while trying to ignore that voice inside my head saying "What does it even matter?"

A few minutes later there was a knock at my door. It was John in his suit, with his many books and legal pad.

"Good morning, sleeping beauty!" he said.

I smiled and opened the door so he could come in.

"What has you cooped up in your room on such a gorgeous day?" he asked.

I feel ugly. I feel fat. I feel rejected by you.

"Nothing," I said.

"I brought something for your spiritual journey," he said.

"Oh?"

He reached inside his jacket pocket and pulled out a small, light-pink booklet.

"This is for you. A friend gave it to me and I've carried it around ever since."

I took the booklet. The cover read, "My Heart—Christ's Home."

"Thank you," I said.

"You don't have to read it right away. But I think it might answer some questions you have."

"Oh, I'll definitely read it."

"Well, Princess, I'm headed to the airport."

"OK. Good to see you."

"Get out of the room and talk to people. Have some fun!"

"Is that what the booklet says to do?"

John laughed. "You'll have to read it to find out!"

We hugged and said good-bye. Just forty-eight hours ago John was just a guy I saw once a year, and now I was pining over him. It was good timing, though, because Simon was getting serious with his girl-friend. Nothing like a new crush to get over an old one.

I removed my security cardigan and flopped on the bed. I flipped to the first page of the booklet. On the inside was a handwritten note. It was dated 7/1/1996. *Wow, he's been carrying this thing around for almost fifteen years*, I thought. I had to shake away the next thought that giving it to me had any meaning beyond "sharing the Word," as they say.

The note read:

To John, A friend in ministry——The Lord of Life has blessed the message this booklet to me. May he reveal his fullness to you in a more blessed way! A friend in Christ, Jim

OK, these guys were serious about this stuff. I turned the page and continued reading: "In his letter to the Ephesians . . ."

I wasn't ready for this right then. It's no wonder God supposedly used big gestures like a burning bush and frogs raining from the sky. The Good Word is *boring*.

I put the booklet in my purse. I'd read it eventually and leave my room eventually, but not today.

16

After Palm Beach, I was totally focused on the conference. Now that John and I had spent some time together, he was more involved in helping me with the conference in an unofficial capacity. The conference was held Thursday through Saturday in mid-February. John was planning to come in on the Saturday before the conference and suggested that we go to church on Sunday. Valentine's Day.

Sunday morning, I followed his directions to the church. It was the oldest one in Falls Church, Virginia. In fact, it was named Falls Church before the town was named Falls Church. For the last month I had been working ten to twelve hours a day every single day. Missing a few hours of work only a few days before the conference was a big deal. But church with John was an even bigger deal.

Planning a conference takes a lot of attention to detail. I think about things other people don't. Getting ready for an outing with John was really no different. There are preparations going on in my head that normal people would think about, such as arriving early. Arriving early ensures that I won't have to approach him already talking to people and won't have to worry about making an awkward entrance. OK, that could be considered normal date behavior (even though this wasn't a date). But I'm the expert, so I go the extra mile. Not only do I need to be there early, but I need to be inside. It's mid-February, and a heavy coat is needed. But what I don't want is to be seen looking fifty pounds heavier. So, the coat is off and draped over my arm when John walks in.

He scoffed when I told him he should wear a suit to church, but there he was wearing a suit.

"Lisa! You're here! You're going to love Yates," he said, referring to the pastor. "I'm so happy you're here today."

"Me too."

"Let's go in and find our seats!"

We walk into the main sanctuary of the church. It was larger than I expected. It seemed to be completely lit by natural light. We chose a pew in the middle center.

"Let's sit on the end," I said.

"Whatever you want!" John said.

I went in to sit down first and let him sit on the very end. It was a prize seat——a place to rest your arm.

The service began with music. And then more music. About twenty minutes of music, actually. Everyone around me was singing, some holding their hands out. These people were serious and it made me uncomfortable. After the music, there was a prayer led by Rector Yates. He had a very kind voice and exhibited a self-deprecating sense of humor. John was right: Yates was good. So good I almost felt guilty that I didn't close my eyes while the hundreds of people around me were in prayer.

I looked at the program. Yates's sermon was titled "Jesus is Supreme. He is God." I wondered if I would ever feel the gravity those were words were meant to have.

After the collection plates went around (I noticed John put in a twenty-dollar bill), Yates began speaking. I guessed he was in his mid-sixties. His voice was very comforting. It was easy to believe what he was saying. He talked about the Epistle to the Hebrews. He said, "This first-century letter or sermon is red hot, still, with passion and power. Some of its passages are like pure oxygen for depleted, exhausted Christians who are in desperate need of revival and restoration."

John elbowed me. "This is for you!" he said.

Yates went on to describe Christians who had fallen from their mental center. A woman who had an affair with a coworker despite being married for thirty years. A man and woman who weren't married but lived together and saw church as just a leisure activity. A woman who considered herself a Christian but found herself restless in her faith and was hesitant to say so.

Yates said, "None of them has grown up into Christian maturity——each of them is still a spiritual baby, and if they fail to grow beyond spiritual infancy, they will not enter into true intimacy with

Christ or into the power of His Holy Spirit who enables us to perse-
vere and sacrifice and embrace the Cross of Christ with fortitude and
peace."

The problem was I didn't feel anything. I often have dreams where
I'm trying to talk to someone and they can't understand me. I'm saying
the words, words I sometimes can't even hear myself say, but the lis-
tener doesn't understand me. I'm frustrated. I felt that way listening
to Yates. The frustration with not being able to communicate had
become my frustration with not "getting it."

I peeked over at John. His eyes were closed and he had fallen asleep.
I elbowed him.

After church I went straight to the office.

"What's going on?" I asked Thomas.

"Just running credit cards. Everyone else is next door stuffing name
badges," he said.

"It's about time. Who's next door?"

"Vincent, Lindsey, the interns, Simon and Karen."

I was on a post-Batman high. I didn't care that Simon and his girlfriend were there.

I set to work on spreadsheets and the millions of other things we
had to do before moving into the hotel the next day. As usual, I heard
Simon before I saw him. He came through the door and sat on the
floor beside my desk.

"Where ya been, Lis'?" he said.

"I went to church with John."

"Oooooooh. How was that?"

"It was good. I like him a lot."

"Yeah, he's good people. Going to church is good. I go with Karen
sometimes. It's a good thing to do. It makes her happy."

"Is that the only reason you go?" I asked.

"Naw, it's good for me. You know, remembering your spirit."

I rolled my eyes. Simon and I had these conversations before. Thanks
to Oprah, "spirituality" these days meant a bubble bath and cashmere
slippers. Not that there's anything wrong with those things.

The next day, John sent me flowers wishing me luck on the conference. I took them with me to the hotel and put them on the nightstand
by my bed.

By Monday night, we were settled into the hotel. Around 9:00 p.m.,
Thomas and I realized there were a couple things that were left behind

at the office. Between volunteers, office staff, and contract staff, we had about seventy-five people at our disposal. But at the end of the day——and it was the end of the day——Thomas and I held it all together. We left the hotel to drive back to the office. When we got there, we found a large box leaning against the building. The conference's closing speaker was famous for using a chalkboard in his speeches. And here it was: a classroom-sized chalkboard that wouldn't fit in any car. We carried it up the stairs and into the office. It was only Monday. We had until Saturday to fix this problem, so there was no point in thinking about it now.

We got the items we needed and drove back to the hotel. On the way I texted to Christine: "Thomas and I went to the office. Driving back now."

Christine was one of my best friends. I met her when she interned for me at my first job in DC. I then hired her as my assistant for my first year at the conference. Since then, I was lucky to have her come back as a volunteer at the conference each year. She was intense, but an integral part of the team that I had relied on year after year.

I quickly got a text back from her. "WHAT? WHY DID YOU TWO LEAVE? WHAT IF SOMETHING WERE TO HAPPEN?"

I actually hadn't thought about it. I suppose Thomas and I were like the president and vice president. The conference was dependent on at least one of us being alive, so not a good idea for us to travel together just before the conference started.

Thankfully, we made it back to the hotel without a scratch. The conference could go on.

With the exception of the usual problems with a conference——late speakers, a dinner ticket or two missing——it went on without a hitch. By Sunday night I was ready to unwind. I had decided to stay an extra night to babysit the chalkboard. The closing speaker had signed it and in order to preserve the signature, I would spray-paint a thin coating of varnish over it every few hours.

John was still staying in the hotel but attending meetings with a friend of his who just happened to be running for president (again). After being witness to the thousands of dollars the conference spent on staff and board members' room service and alcohol tabs, I decided it was perfectly fine for me to order a few in-room movies. I asked John, a movie buff, for recommendations.

"I'll come by your room in 10 minutes!" he texted back.

A few minutes later there was a knock on my door. "Princess! I'm here to assist you with movie night!"

"Well, it should be easy. I haven't seen any new movies."

He grabbed the remote and scrolled through the options. "What do you like? Drama, comedy, romantic comedy?"

"Not really into Julia Roberts–type romantic comedies. I like drama but don't want anything too serious."

"OK, here are my recommendations. For something funny—*Zombieland*. Don't worry, it's more silly than scary. And *An Education*. It's not a traditional love story and it's great. Carey Mulligan is fantastic in her role."

"OK, sounds like a plan."

"I have to go to a business dinner, but I'll come back to catch the ending of one of your movies."

Now this was a plan. I knew what "let's just stay in and watch a movie" meant in college. Did baby boomers like John use that line for the same purpose?

John left and I settled in to watch *An Education* first. Thirty minutes into the movie, I couldn't help but read into John's recommendation. The movie was about a worldly man who has a love affair with a young woman nearly half his age.

Was this a not-so-subtle hint? Or just a movie recommendation?

Next came *Zombieland*. About an hour in, John came back to my room, as promised.

"Oh, you're on *Zombieland*! It's hilarious," he said.

He took off his shoes and sat on the couch. I sat back down on the other end, holding a pillow over my lap. I delighted in his boyish laughter when a particularly gruesome kill happened on screen.

When the movie was over, we talked for a few minutes. He then gave me a hug and left. I wasn't sad that nothing had happened between us. I was just happy to have that feeling of butterflies again.

By April, the post-conference duties were done and things were slow. John was in town for work and suggested we do a postmortem happy hour. I was on edge all day. To make matters worse, I had been exchanging e-mails for most of the afternoon with Chris, my ex-boyfriend. He had a contract job in the area for a few months and wanted to have dinner that night. For some reason I could never say no to him. Oh, who am I kidding: I wasn't able to say no to any guy. If I weren't overweight and an introvert, I'd probably be in Samantha Jones territory.

John arrived at the office close to 5:00 p.m. I invited Thomas and Liz to join us at Austin Grill, a Tex-Mex place nearby in Old Town. By the time we were all ready to leave the office, John was standing outside waiting for us. As I locked the office door behind us, John called out, "What a vision in hot pink!"

Despite it being April, it was still coat weather in DC. I hated it because I thought coats hid the weight I had lost so far. I faced the door and rolled my eyes. It was like he could hone in on whatever I didn't want him to notice.

When we got to the restaurant, we grabbed a booth and ordered drinks. We talked about what could be done differently, what went right, and general conference gossip. I was also keenly aware that this was the first time Thomas and Liz were sitting with me and John knowing that I really liked him.

After two rounds, John asked for the check.

"I have to drive down to Hot Springs tonight. I am not looking forward to it," he said.

"Why are you going there?" I asked.

"It's a Christian mens' retreat. I go to it every year. It's a great event; I just have to get through the drive."

After John graciously paid the bill, we all went our separate ways. I was buzzed from the two drinks and didn't want show up at Chris's hotel that way. Or drive on the Beltway during rush hour. As I sat in my car, I decided to call John.

"Hi again!" I said.

"Hello there!"

"How's the drive going?"

"Boring, as predicted."

"I'm just sitting in my car until my two girly drinks wear off. Also, I don't want to meet my ex for dinner half drunk."

"Well, it depends on what you want to get out of it!"

"Nothing from him! I need a nice guy like you."

"But I'm too old for you!"

"No, you're not!"

"I'm like twenty years older than you."

He said it with humor, but even in my buzzed state I knew it was his way of brushing me off. There was no point in replying that he was actually only fifteen years older. I wished him luck on his weekend with a bunch of Christian men as I started the car and drove to meet my atheist ex-boyfriend. Feeling dejected, I knew what was going to happen that night. I wouldn't say no. I also knew how much it hurt to admit it.

17

That summer I made my usual trek to Palm Beach. I was able to tack on a trip to the National Rifle Association's annual meeting in Charlotte at the beginning of the trip, giving me almost a full month away from the office.

Being alone at a conference wasn't fun. I was used to having Simon or Thomas as my armor. I was quickly reminded of school field trips, when I was the only one who didn't pair up with a best friend or group of friends. Sometimes I could pair up temporarily with another loner, but it didn't last. On top of that, I didn't have the cool sack lunch like the others. Every week my mother gave me a check to take to the cafeteria. She paid for my sister and I for the week. (Years later, my sister thought we were poor enough to qualify for free lunch, not knowing I had taken the money to the lunch lady every week.)

So, when it came time to bring a lunch on a field trip, I didn't have a cool lunch box or cool lunch items like chips and fruit roll-ups. It seemed I always ended up with a sandwich with at least one end piece, fifty cents so I could buy a Diet Coke (though there almost never was a Coke machine once we got there), and the most humiliating part—carrying my lunch in an empty bread bag.

Thankfully, I got through the conference and was on the road early Sunday morning so I could get to Palm Beach with minimal stops.

After settling in for a few days, I had the idea for a column that would highlight conservatives' pop culture interests, hopefully making them more appealing to the masses. Having run the conference for four years, I already had a pretty good bank of people I could interview.

But first I wanted to reach out to activist and pop culture nut Andrew Breitbart. After an hour-long conversation (there were only hour-long conversations with Andrew), I was convinced that this was going to be a great column. I was itching to do something creative in addition to my event-planning duties, and this would be a perfect fit.

It was also a good opportunity to pick John's brain about the questions to ask. He didn't disappoint.

Dear Conference Cutie,

OK—here is my advice on your nascent column and your expanded service to the VRWC. Because of who you are, you are getting the "full Batman treatment"—but you are under no obligation to heed any of this advice. Even though it's solid platinum.

What the movement (and movement leaders) need more than any additional topical analysis is an outlet or device to humanize the personalities of its major activists. Anything that reveals a sense of humor, irony, self-reflection, poetry, child-like innocence or savage wit would make political or cultural warriors more appealing—and thus more persuasive—to the masses. Think about those individuals whose opinions you value. Are any of them unrelentingly angry? Humorless? Dull?

Most movement activists are so focused on the issue / battle du jour that they bury these qualities in themselves. Or actively seek to disguise them for fear of appearing "non-serious." But by de-humanizing themselves they become, over time, "school marm-ish"—and instant excuses to change the channel whenever they appear.

Why is there such rabid interest in the performances at the annual White House Correspondent's Dinner or Gridiron or Alfalfa Club soirees? Because serious players have a serious need to see serious players be non-serious.

This is not an invitation to frivolity. Rather, an appeal to a leader to offer a brief glimpse of what they're like on Saturday mornings with their children or grandchildren. Or what they daydream about when not saving the world. Or simply how they re-charge their creative batteries.

Batman

He got it.

Naturally, I started with Ann Coulter, the conservative movement's most famous and witty woman. Coincidentally, a friend and mentor.

After I got back from Palm Beach, the grumbling about the gays started. For years the conference had been home to all facets of the conservative movement. That's what made it the largest conference in terms of attendance and sponsors. However, in late 2010, a group of social conservatives decided that a group that represented gay conservatives should no longer be welcomed. While only a handful of past sponsors participated in a "boycott" of the conference, at least a dozen groups that had never participated in the conference signed on, elevating the boycott's profile beyond it's real effect on the conference's bottom line.

A board vote confirmed that the gay group would be allowed to participate. I was someone who lived and breathed the conference, but I never had the opportunity to speak to a single board member about the real effects of the boycott. The truth was, there was no boycott to speak of. As the conference grew closer, we had more money, attendees, speakers, and sponsors than ever before. In essence, the only reason to oust the gay conservative group was because a small group of people plain didn't want gays there. But, as I had often seen in DC, it wasn't about the facts, it was about the power. A handful of board members wanted to prove they had the power to ban a group from "their" conference.

The chairman, who I had supported for years, was likely to retire, and I started to think about what the conference would look like without him. Did I want to be there? Was there anywhere else I could go? Was the movement changing, or just the conference?

As always, I reached out to John for advice.

Hi Lisa,

I know it feels like you're drowning in your workload. The reason you're getting all these assignments is because the chairman believes that you can do them—in an environment that doesn't afford him a ton of other people to trust.

But on a more fundamental level, you seem like you're still not pursuing a life dream that makes you happy. Try something radical—pray this prayer and heed its answer:

"A Prayer for Joy:

Help me, O God,
To listen to what it is that makes my heart glad and to follow
* where it leads.*
May joy, not guilt,
Your voice, not the voices of others,
Your will, not my willfulness,
be the guides that lead me to my vocation.
Help me to unearth the passions of my heart that lay buried in
* my youth.*
And help me to go over that ground again and again,
until I can hold in my hands, hold and treasure, Your calling on
* my life."*

Your calling can be a family, a career, a mission overseas—just be
honest with yourself about what you WANT, and then use your smarts
(and your connections) to chase after THAT.

John

I read it over and over. I wish I had the clarity to understand my
calling. Since I was ten, I said I wanted to be a writer. Then when I
met a former coworker with four kids and a seemingly perfect life, I
wanted to be a stay-at-home mother who wrote on the side. As I got
older, the options for a calling seemed to shrink. Why would God help
me? John's words were perfect on paper, but their message seemed out
of reach to me.

John arrived a few days before the conference to get settled and
help with any last-minute "intern duties." Like the year before (and
the year before that), Thomas and I were working twelve to fourteen
hours a day. Last year I had given myself a few hours away from the
office to go to church with John. This year I left the office to meet John
for dinner at the hotel and give him a tour of the revamped setup. We
were at the same venue but had switched things up to accommodate
the growing crowds and an improved VIP space.

After the tour, we went to the hotel restaurant. When John put on
his reading glasses to look at the menu, I couldn't help but smile. I
felt young around him, which was unusual for me. Often I felt like
I was ahead of everyone else in terms of experience and thinking.

But with John I felt like the student. It was comfortable, but also exhilarating.

The waitress came to the table to take our order. "The young lady first," John said.

"I'll have the chicken fingers," I said.

"And you, sir?" the waitress asked.

"I'll have the meatloaf and mashed potatoes."

I snickered to myself. I had ordered the typical kid's meal and he had ordered the typical dad's meal. Thankfully, he didn't insist I also order milk.

After dinner, John and I walked through the lobby just as my friend Christine and her father were coming in. Christine was my assistant during my first conference, and now she came back every year to corral the volunteers and help me. If Thomas was my right hand, Christine was my left hand. I couldn't do the event without them. The bonus gift I got with Christine was her dad, who had also come to help out that year.

There the four of us were in the lobby, Christine meeting John for the first time after hearing me gush over him. Christine's dad and John shook hands.

"So, you're here for the conference?" John asked.

"Oh, I'm just here to do whatever Christine tells me to do," her dad said.

"Ha! That makes two of us. You can barely see the marks from the collar Lisa has me wear."

Everyone laughed, and it was at that moment I noticed the two men might be around the same age. Christine and her dad went to check in. It was just past 8:00 p.m. and, sadly, I needed to get back to the office.

"Oh Conference Princess, I have something for you!" John said.

"What is it? What is it?" I asked excitedly.

He reached into his computer bag and pulled out a silver drawstring bag. "For the princess, a crown."

I reached into the bag. Inside was a silver and rhinestone crown. I lit up. I had once mentioned that all I needed was a crown.

"It's so fancy! I was just expecting a plastic one!" I said.

"No, nothing but the best, baby!"

I left the hotel and couldn't help but smile the entire drive back to the office.

Once the conference was underway, most of the controversy about the gay conservative group disappeared, part of the reason being that there was always some other news that was made at the conference. This year, there was one man who could easily draw attention away from the gays and toward his head of glorious hair: Donald Trump.

After numerous phone calls, we were set on an arrival time and the person who would introduce him: me. I decided to give a more serious introduction than the one I gave Rush a few years before.

The conference motored along. The board had voted in a new chairman and several new board members, including John. But something about that weekend made it feel like the last time. Backstage just before the closing speech, I talked to Simon's mother. She was also a board member and had been a mainstay of the conference for years. She worked at a prominent lobbying organization and seemed to know everyone—some friends and some enemies. I was always grateful that as busy as she was, she always took my calls.

"Were you able to grab a sandwich earlier?" I asked

"Yes, what about you?" she said

"No, I don't eat sandwiches. I actually don't eat that much during the day."

"Lisa, that's not good."

"No, it's fine. I don't know if you've noticed, but I've lost a lot of weight over the last two years."

"I have noticed. I'm so proud of you!" she said.

"Thank you. It's been tough, but it's something I needed to do."

She began to tear up. "You look great. I'm just so proud of you."

I was surprised by her emotion but touched that she cared so much.

"Do you think this will be our last conference together?"

"It might be. I could use a break," she said.

During the closing speech, Thomas and I sat just off stage. We had now done five conferences together. After putting 362 days into planning the conference, this one was about to end. Each year seemed to go quicker and quicker. I reached for my phone and took our photo.

After the conference ended, things didn't immediately seem that different. The former chairman still kept an office in our building. One afternoon, the new chairman was supposed to come in for a meeting with all the staff.

At 1:00 p.m., we all gathered at the conference table. The new chairman wasn't there.

"Unfortunately, the chairman can't be here, so he'll be calling by phone," said the new executive director, a Gordon Gekko wannabe with slicked-back hair.

A few seconds later the phone rang. The chairman gave the typical "all is well, exciting things are ahead, no one is getting fired" speech and then we all went back to our offices.

On my way home from work, I called John to get the real scoop.

"Yes, there will be changes. They're going with a leaner staff," he said.

"What does that mean for me and Thomas?" I asked.

"You're not going anywhere for the foreseeable future. They'll need at least six months to decide what they're doing about the conference."

"What about Thomas?"

"That, I don't know."

I hung up. Sometimes talking to John brought more questions than answers.

Later that week, I decided my best defense was to give the new chairman all the information I had. I was sure he was getting information from others on the board, including those who wanted the gay group gone. Many of them were too cowardly to stand up to the old chairman, who was still a force in DC, so instead they blamed me for the controversy they manufactured by ginning up fake boycotters.

I sent a twenty-five-page memo to the new and old chairmen, basically giving them all the information on the increase in sponsors, revenue, and attendees, my defense of letting all groups into the conference, and how to continue to grow the conference.

The next day we held a meeting with all the sponsors. I always dreaded the postmortem meeting because everyone bitched about the littlest things. The location of their booth was too cold. The hotel took too long to reset their meeting room. Their panel was cut short. This year, though, I knew it was going to be about the gays when I noticed the heads of various sponsors showing up rather than just sending their event or communications staffers.

Several of them had their grandstanding moments against the gays, while the executive director of the gay group sat there listening to them. Finally, the outgoing chairman called on him to speak. He stood up, looking directly at the people who spoke out against him. He said, "All we wanted to do was be part of this conference. We're conservatives. We're pro-life. We have not done anything to compromise the conference. We didn't ask for anything but to be there at our booth."

After the meeting, the new chairman came over to several of us staff members. Thomas introduced himself. "Hi, I'm Lisa's assistant. I've been with her for four years."

"Very good. Nice to meet you," he answered.

The next day I did something I hadn't done in nearly five years. I went to a job interview. Christine was working there as a news analyst during an overnight shift. It wasn't ideal, but the money was good. I didn't think it could hurt to check out my options.

When I got back to the office, Thomas and I went to lunch. I think he was a little put off by the fact that I went to an interview. It didn't matter that it wasn't a job that I wanted. He must have been wondering where it would leave him.

On our way back from lunch, we saw the executive director.

"Hey, can you come by my office at three?"

"Sure, no problem," I said.

I figured it had to do with the files I had compiled for him. Since he was new to the organization and the conference, I wanted to prove that I knew my stuff. I compiled at least a dozen folders containing documents explaining the various aspects of the conference.

I walked into his office. We made small talk for a few minutes and he asked for my advice about a media issue. Then he said the last thing I was expecting to hear.

"We're going to have to let you go."

I didn't remember much after that. Thomas was getting fired, too. I was scheduled to go on my vacation two days later. Now I was being told I had to pack my stuff and leave as soon as possible. Five years of increasingly successful conferences meant nothing.

I walked back over to my office and went straight to the bathroom. I couldn't even look at Thomas. I couldn't warn him. I heard the intern tell him that the ED wanted to talk to him. Less than ten minutes later, Thomas was back.

We barely talked when he came back to the office. I was crying and packing up all the useless things that accumulated in my office over the years. Weird kitschy items. Photos with friends and speakers. I left the photo of me, the old chairman, and Rush. I had no savings, and the severance was minimal. I barely even had any photos from the conference because I was always focused on getting photos for everyone else.

As I carried a box of stuff to my car, I passed a coworker. She said "hello," then quickly averted her eyes because she realized what was happening. I just gave her an angry look and kept walking.

My car was packed up. It was time for Thomas and I to say good-bye. We were still too stunned to say much. We made plans to see each other the next day.

I texted a couple people. Everyone was stunned. Then I thought of John. He said I had at least six months. I was so angry. Was it possible he just didn't know, or did he know and not tell me? And Simon's mother. When did she know? Was that why she started crying during our conversation backstage?

My identity was gone. I had nothing left. No boyfriend or husband to go home to. No dog to greet me at the door. I had been fired from another job.

The next day was surreal. It was Friday. Christine had just finished her night shift but came over to my house. Thomas came by, too. It was time to work on our resumes. I also had to decide whether to still go on vacation. The conference circuit was growing in the conservative movement, and the handful of people I had talked to seemed to think lots of organizations would want to hire me.

I decided that for my own mental health, I would still drive down to Florida. I was also due to visit my dad and sister.

Later that afternoon my phone rang. It was Simon's mom. I let it go to voicemail. I knew I would eventually have to talk to people, but right then I just wanted to spend the day with Thomas and Christine.

While Christine and I went to Target, Thomas stayed at the house. Once we got back, Christine was the first to leave. Around 10:00 p.m., Thomas decided to leave. It was a weird good-bye. We had worked every day together full time for the last three years. We sometimes hung out on the weekends. Now we were saying good-bye for an inde-terminate time.

After Thomas left, I noticed a beige coin purse on top of the mag-azines that Christine left for me to take on vacation. I unzipped it and inside were a couple pieces of Dove chocolates and $300 in cash. There was also a note from Christine. "Everything will be ok! Enjoy your vacation!"

I was so angry for dedicating the last five years of my life to that conference but so thankful for the friendships it gave me. Thomas and Christine meant more to me than any photos.

Once I got to Palm Beach, I knew I had made the right decision.

I would have driven myself crazy if I stayed in the DC area. Also, the news of me being let go was set to be in the *Washington Times* that Monday. Once I saw the story was posted online Sunday night, I posted it on Twitter and Facebook. There were a couple follow-up stories, including one by a fringe media outlet that titled their story, "Conservative conference dumps director."

Most people seemed to think I had left on my own. When they asked, "What are you doing next?" my answer was, "I don't know."

Some people thought I had moved back to Florida. I considered it and set up a meeting with a conservative organization—a magazine— while I was down there. Unfortunately, my contact there canceled the day before. It was starting. All of the contacts I had made over the years were no longer returning calls and e-mails. Some ignored me because they didn't have any advice or jobs to offer. Others because I was no longer of any use to them.

Finally, after a week of being in Palm Beach, I called John.

"So, are you working on your tan?" he said.

"Yes, and looking for a job."

"Well, what do you want to do?"

I was so annoyed with John for acting like everything was great. As if I had the option of waiting for my dream job. "I don't know. People just seem to think I'm an event planner," I said.

"I don't think that's true. You have a stellar reputation in the movement."

"No, I *had* a stellar reputation until I got fired. Again."

"You'll be fine."

"You don't know that. You said I had six months. He got rid of me and Thomas after just a few weeks. We never even talked to the new chairman. I'll be out of my severance in two months."

"And with your vacation pay, it's close to three months."

"No, it's not, because vacation pay only covers my bills for this month. If I would have been fired two weeks later, I'd be in the same position."

"You just need to decide what you want to do and pursue that," he said.

He wasn't hearing me. This was no longer about deciding what I wanted. Soon it would be about taking anything I could get. This was about him telling me I had six months before a decision would be made and then being blindsided. I didn't know if his optimism about my situation was because he genuinely believed I would be OK or if he was trying to make up for misleading me.

When I hung up, I was still angry. It would be several months before we would talk again. Even superheroes were no match for the disintegrating job market.

When I got back from Palm Beach, I immersed myself in the job market, spending several hours a day looking for nonpolitical jobs. Every once in a while I would come across a political position that could be a good fit. Mostly I wanted to separate myself from anyone connected to the conference drama, including Simon and John.

Over the next several months I was able to pick up a few side projects. I helped Simon's stepfather with research for his book. I did logistics for a women's conference with seventy-five attendees. I sat behind actor Robert Davi's booth at the National Italian American Foundation's annual gala and hocked his *Davi Sings Sinatra* CDs. In just six months, I went from running a conference of ten thousand to being someone's booth bitch.

In order to pay my bills each month and not rack up even more debt, I didn't say no to any paid opportunity. Just after Thanksgiving, a friend offered me part-time work at her public relations firm. Shortly after that, political drama with the gay conservative organization caused them to look for a new board chair. I was unanimously elected as the interim chair. As far as dating went, perhaps that wasn't my best-laid plan.

A few days into the new year, I sent an e-mail to every professional and personal contact I had, detailing the type of position I wanted and the skills I possessed. It was interesting to see who wrote back. Most didn't. But, there were a few rays of hope. A friend wrote that she knew of an open position at a nonprofit, economic-focused group in DC. She said it was likely below my level of experience, but that it would be a good transition position. It involved press relations, event planning, and some administrative work. It sounded perfect. Sure, I wasn't ecstatic about the administrative work, but it was a full-time job and my contract work was running out soon.

I told Margaret the job sounded great and I would appreciate the recommendation. A few days later, I heard from the organization's chief of staff and we set up a time for an in-person interview.

Since I was driving into DC for the interview and traffic there is notoriously unpredictable, I left very early and arrived over an hour before the interview was to start. Their office was in a well-known building of conservative heavy hitters. One author described the building as housing more conservative thinkers than some European countries.

The interview went well and we made tentative plans for a conference call so I could also interview with the director of the organization's New York office.

18

After the interview process concluded, I was eager to know if a decision had been made. After ten months of unemployment, I was used to applying for jobs and then never hearing back. If employees treated customers and clients the same way hiring managers treat applicants, they would all be fired.

It was January 30 and I was alone in the PR firm where I was doing temp work. My friend had a lunch date with a guy she met at the New Hampshire primary. I knew of him since he was the producer of a political TV show, but not enough to have an opinion on their encounter in a stairwell in a New Hampshire hotel.

Suddenly an e-mail came from the chief of staff of the organization I had interviewed with a few weeks prior.

Lisa—

Thanks for taking the time to meet with us over the last few weeks.
I have really enjoyed getting to know more about you and what you
might be able to bring to the e21 family. It is my pleasure to offer you
a position with e21 . . .

I was so overcome with happiness and relief that I couldn't finish reading the e-mail. Light seemed to overflow from the two office windows. My heart felt full and lifted. For the first time in twenty years, I clasped my hands together and thanked God.

And right then I realized this was the moment. Finally, after all of these years, I felt God's hand in my life. Even when I didn't accept Him, He accepted and protected me.

I started my new job the week the conservative conference started. It was a big deal to me that I had found a full-time job before the conference. I was also willing to reconnect with John. The Sunday before the conference, he e-mailed suggesting we go to church and then brunch afterward. I had not yet shared my story of feeling God come into my heart.

I met John in the church lobby. I was eager to see him and eager to get the gossip on the conference.

"Does anyone miss me?" I asked.

"Are you kidding? It's a cluster-you-know-what. When I arrived on Friday for the walk-through at the hotel, there were four new people with me. As we were walking through, I was giving them a list of things they needed to do. When they were to the point of being over-whelmed, I reminded them that in the previous years, all these tasks were done by one person."

"No one realizes it because I made it look easy," I said. "They were never involved. As Rumsfeld said, they don't know what they don't know."

"And to top it off, the conference director won't even be at the conference."

"What?"

And at that moment, the choir started and the service began.

"I'll give you all the juicy details at brunch," John whispered.

My mind was reeling. What could have happened? Was it all the drama of not allowing the gay group? I thought back to the last con-versation I had with the new directorbefore he replaced mer. We were at my last conference in 2011. He had just finished moderating a panel.

"Thank you again for putting me on this panel," he said after giving me a hug.

"Oh, you're welcome. I needed someone who could corral the other panelists," I said.

"I know this has been a tough year for you. I'm dealing with the old mindset over at the institute and I need to get out of there."

I knew his former boss was one of the board members leading the charge against the gay organization. Maybe he pushed back and they didn't want him at the conference and saying the wrong thing to the media.

I looked at the church program. Today's sermon was titled "No Condemnation." This was going to be interesting.

The rector said, "But in spite of this, many believers still struggle with feelings of condemnation because of their own sin and failure before God to live as Christ calls us."

I elbowed John and raised my eyebrow. I recalled another board member, a person many people told me was an alcoholic, who was also vocal about ousting me and the gay conservatives.

He continued:

> "Any of us who has begun to follow Christ and grows in our sense of what He asks of us, is well aware of how often we fall short of Christ's call. Many Christians wrestle with ongoing or periodic disappointment at how selfish they know themselves to be, or how they have failed God or others. Sometimes we ignore Christ's most challenging commandments, or we attempt to obey and fail miserably. Perhaps we are living with one foot on the world's pathway and the other on Christ's path, and these paths head in two very different directions. So we make little progress in the Christian life. Even the most sensitive Christians, the most committed, can fall so far short of Christ's rigorous demands or his example, that we struggle with failure and disappointment, and we lose our sense of value before God."

I spent many days and nights thinking about my value in the political world. Even as I began my new job, I knew the title couldn't compare to my previous position. I had failed in my personal life and work life. I was worried that I would soon be failing as a Christian. I already knew so many Christians who seemed to be failing and watched as they publicly condemned others for doing the same.

A month after receiving God, I wasn't yet ready to share my story with others because of my pride. I was dreading the "I told you so" smirks and remarks. I still wanted others, including John, to know that I was continuing the journey, though. One afternoon I e-mailed him.

Batman,

What's a good version of the Bible to get? Perhaps more "yous" than "thous."

Lisa

I quickly heard back from him.

Shipping one to you tomorrow!!

Bibles R Us,

John

A few days later, I received a package. Inside was a Bible with a pink leather cover. It was perfect! Inside was a letter.

Dear Lisa,

For my newest sister in Christ, a Bible as stylish as the sista' herself. Please find enclosed a "New Living Translation" Study Bible (without all the thee's and thou's). Some cool things about one of these that aren't always obvious:

This is a "study Bible"—meaning that at the front of each is a one-page primer on the chapter's author or times that does more to help my understanding of what follows than any pastor I've had. AND there are a lot of VERY helpful footnotes that explain the action and underlying meaning of a lot of passages. (The footnotes are oftentimes more helpful than the verse.)

This is a "red letter edition Bible"—meaning that the actual quotes from Jesus are highlighted in red in the New Testament.

The maps in the back are way huge cheats to understand both Biblical action—and modern day politics.

- *The "concordance" at the back is Biblical terminology for "index." If you want to find a person or a passage on a specific topic, simply look it up alphabetically and, voila!*
- *The salvation passage that most everyone knows (and that Tim Tebow wears under his eyes at football games), John 3:16, is key. But Ephesians 2:8-10 is more descriptive of where most believers are on a day-to-day basis. (I've put the ribbon there for you.)*
- *This is a pretty Bible, but NEVER be afraid to write in it. A "good Bible" is a marked-up Bible. Trust me, they make more.*

I'm so excited to share this with you!!! It's never too early or too late if you have a question about anything . . .

VERY Sincerely,
Your Batman

19

A few months into my new job, I was planning their biannual monetary policy conference in New York. John was also in the city that weekend, so plans were made for him to take me to my first Broadway show. After years of doing all the planning in my professional and personal life, John's e-mail with the details for my extended trip was a welcome change.

Broadway Babe,

Here follows the fun details for your "first night on Broadway"!!!

1. Lodging: When you wrap up at the Yale Club, you can check into your suite at the Marriott Marquis, 1535 Broadway (the corner of 45th St. & 7th Ave.).

When you arrive at the Marquis, take the elevators to the 8th Floor (lobby), proceed to the "Elite" check-in desk, announce your name and they'll hand you the key to your suite. Head upstairs, relax and enjoy the view!

2. Dinner: We're dining at Sardi's at 6:00 PM with Floyd & Colleen—northern Italian TDF. It's one block from the hotel.

3. Your First Broadway Show: We're going to see "The Phantom of the Opera" at the Majestic Theatre at 8:00 PM!!! (It's right next to Sardi's.) Even if you've seen a traveling company,

nothing beats the staging of Broadway. Big music, big
romance, Floyd & Colleen love it and it's a "life check-mark"
for any Broadway hit list. I hope I guessed right!

4. After Show Drinks: There are dozens of great delis and bars all
   around us, as well as the revolving restaurant / bar atop our
   Marquis with spectacular views of Manhattan. It's your night,
   you can have any treat you want!

I'll let you know if there are any last minute changes—you do the
same. This will be a blast!

John

When I arrived at the Marriott Marquis suite he had gotten me, I
was blown away by the view. I had the perfect view of Times Square
and the 2012 New Year's Eve ball. I looked at the floor-to-ceiling windows in my thirtieth-floor suite. I was so thankful for all the positive
changes so far that year.

That evening I was wearing a teal wrap dress. It covered my arms
and highlighted my more attractive assets—cleavage, eyes, and waist.
Being in New York, I knew it was more chic to wear black, but when
dressing up I liked jewel tones. Also, it allowed me to wear nude kitten
heels that were far more comfortable than the mile-high shoes most
women wore.

Just after 6:00 p.m., there was a knock at the door. I opened the
door and there John stood in a suit and vibrant purple tie.

"You're looking radiant in teal! Are you ready for your night on
Broadway?" he said.

"I am! And thanks for the room. Come look at my view!"

"Only the best for baby! Before I forget, I have a gift for you."

"I like gifts!"

"This is the daily devotional I read every day. Each day it's just a
short story that ties together with a verse or message. It takes less than
five minutes of your day," he said.

"Oh, thanks!" I said, taking the small booklet and putting it on the
nightstand. "We better get going. Floyd is already at the restaurant."

"Sardi's is only a block away, so it won't take us long to walk over.
Shall we go?"

"We shall."

When we arrived at Sardi's, Floyd was standing outside. I hadn't seen him since I was in Palm Beach, so it was great to see him.

"Hey, Boop! Give me a hug," Floyd said.

"Hey! Where's Colleen?"

"Oh, she's on her way. She's always late, so let's go ahead and get our table."

The restaurant was packed. After everyone ordered a drink, Colleen came in. I immediately felt inadequate when she breezed through in black crepe pants, heels, and a shimmery leopard blouse. My teal dress felt loud, not radiant. I felt like the kid sitting at the adult's table.

As we finished dinner, the men started jockeying for the bill. It was quite a performance by the two of them.

After dinner, we walked to the theater and took our seats for *Phantom of the Opera*.

After the show, we headed over to a bar on the top floor of a hotel in Times Square, the Radisson maybe? By that time, I was just trying to keep up with everyone as they weaved through the throngs of people swarming Times Square.

After drinks and dessert, I said good-bye to Colleen and Floyd and John and I walked back to the hotel. It was 1:00 a.m. and he insisted on walking me back to my room. This was his chance. If he wanted to pursue more than a friendship, now was his time to show me. Instead, we hugged at the door and said good night. All I wanted was to be wanted by him. Or anyone.

As I lay in bed, I thought of Christine's song in *Phantom of the Opera*.

> *Think of me, think of me fondly*
> *When we've said goodbye*
> *Remember me once in a while*
> *Please promise me, you'll try*

I reached for my phone and sent a message to another man I knew. Maybe it wasn't John's attention that I needed, but any man's attention. I knew the man I was messaging didn't really care about me. It was after 1:00 a.m. The meaning was clear. He was either asleep or not interested in talking that night. I eventually went to sleep wanting more from someone. Anyone.

John and I kept in touch after New York, but I was increasingly annoyed with his growing involvement in the conference. I hated that he always felt the need to tell me how well the conference planning was going. The gentlemanly thing to do would be to say, "It's nothing without you!"

It was clear that John's first priority was the conference. I had made peace with not being more than a friend to John, but the more he insisted how great everything was without me, the more I didn't even think of him as a friend.

PRESTON
the Quaker

20

It was December 2010. I was still director of the conservative conference. We had a short break during Christmas before Thomas and I came back and worked sixteen-hour days. Our sanity until then was dependent on the fact that everyone took the last two weeks of the year off. Sure I would be checking my e-mail and thinking about banquet orders, but I got to take a break from going into the office and, more importantly, answering my office phone.

There's just something about holidays that makes you want a significant other. Just after Thanksgiving I joined a Christian dating site. I was trying to come to terms with the fact that John the Evangelical wasn't interested in me, but thought finding someone like him might finally put me over the edge in becoming a committed Christian.

I joined the most popular Christian dating site. Signing up for only one month seemed rather ambitious, so I got the three-month package. I tried to be honest about myself. I used flattering photos but chose "full-figured" for body type. Let's face it: every shorty-pants man can say he's five eight when he's really five four, but if a woman isn't honest about her body flaws, we're the liars.

My profile description was short and casual.

I'm originally from Florida and have been in the D.C. area for over 12 years. I'm politically conservative, but generally don't bring work home with me. I like going to the movies, exploring the D.C. area, reading, walking, cooking (I'm southern and Italian, so yeah, I'm a good cook), among many other things. Friends tell me I'm witty, my

mom says I'm pretty, and ex-boyfriends say I'm the one who got
away ;)

I'm looking for a combination of "Ron Swanson" and Bruce Campbell.
Must like football and my cooking/baking, be affectionate, be a Christian, and be able to teach me something new.

The first response I got was from a guy named Preston. I learned
that online dating wasn't as anonymous as I had hoped it would be.

"Hi! I follow you on Twitter. I'm a big fan of the conference," he
wrote.

I didn't know what to think. He didn't mention anything about the
fact that we were communicating on an online dating site. He seemed
to just be another conservative boy who wasn't interested in me but in
my proximity to political stars. Admittedly, I was the Forrest Gump of
the conservative movement and found myself in the midst of a lot of
interesting moments, but I had zero interest in dating anyone who was
only impressed by that part of my life.

I politely responded that it was nice to hear from him and that I
hoped he would attend the conference in February.

A few days later, I tweeted that I was interested in buying a new
digital camera and asked if anyone had any recommendations. Within
a few minutes, Preston was sending message after message about cam-
eras. After a string of messages between us, he surmised that this particular one was the best and it came in pink. Apparently, he knew me
better than the paragraph or so I had put on the dating site.

While I was visiting my mom and stepdad for Christmas in Williamsburg, Preston and I started playing Words with Friends. He frequently messaged me on their chat feature.

"Any luck on the online dating?" he wrote.

"Nope, nothing yet."

"I'm surprised there's not a hundred guys at your door!"

Really? Then why aren't you asking me out?

"Well, I guess I'm just not the right type for online dating," I told him.

"That can't be. You're beautiful, smart, and successful. You're out
of my league that's for sure," he said.

I'm not that great at reading cues from men, but men will generally
tell you who they are. The cheaters say something like, "Women are
my weakness." The alcoholics say, "I need to cut back on my drinking."
Every other issue is covered by, "You're out of my league." Depending

on what the issue is (too short, underemployed, intimidated by beautiful, conservative Twitter-famous women), a girl can learn to work around on it.

After Christmas, I left Williamsburg and made a quick stop at home. I switched out dirty laundry for clean and headed to my favorite resort hotel in National Harbor, Maryland. My friends there were giving me a great deal on the presidential suite . . . as long as I was out by New Year's Eve.

The room was fantastic. It had a large living room with a wall of windows that looked over the Potomac River and across to Old Town, Alexandria. There was a fireplace in front of plush couches that were perfect for reading. The bathroom had a Jacuzzi tub and a shower with a hundred different jets and settings. The kitchen and dining room barely attracted my attention.

After a great night's sleep, I visited the hotel spa for a facial. While there, Preston texted and asked if he could take me to dinner as a "thank you" for everything I'd done for the conservative movement. I obliged and told him I wanted to try the seafood restaurant in the hotel. Since I had boasted about my room, I gave him the room number and said I'd give him a quick tour before dinner.

"Sounds like a plan. I've made a reservation for 7:00 p.m., so I'll come by your room at 6:45 p.m.," he responded.

I was impressed. As an event planner, I adore when men take the initiative to make a reservation rather than show up shocked that other people also want to eat dinner at dinnertime.

At 6:45 p.m. on the dot, there was a knock on my door. I looked through the peephole and saw that Preston was facing away from the door. When I opened the door, he immediately started grinning. "I made a point of being right on time," he said.

"And I appreciate it!" I said. "Come in and I'll give you a quick tour."

He walked in and took off his coat. He was in a dark blue suit and expensive-looking shoes. He may have been an inch or so shorter than me. If life was a Dickens novel, he might have been described as *portly*. In online dating terms, perhaps he would describe himself as *cuddly*.

"I brought something for you," he said. "Just something silly."

He reached into his pocket and pulled out a little stuffed cow. I recognized it as the one Chick-fil-A sold around the holidays. Somehow I had accumulated two or three of these little cows, but I didn't dare tell him since he seemed so proud of his find.

"Oh, that's so cute!" I said.

"I know you like Chick-fil-A, so when I was there a few days ago I had to get it for you," he said, smiling like a boy who had just pleased his mother.

"I do love Chick-fil-A. I'll put him on the bed so he'll be waiting for me," I said. "We better get going so we're not late for dinner."

On our way out, he went to grab his coat. "Oh, you can leave it here and come back to get it after dinner," I told him.

We took the elevator down to the restaurant. Our table wasn't quite ready, so we went to the bar to get a drink first. It was a trendy sea-food restaurant. The bar area had tiny leather chairs with high arms. I noticed that the chair was an uncomfortable fit for him. Even though I still had a significant amount of weight to lose, I was past the daily worry of not fitting into chairs. Sure, some were more comfortable than others, but I no longer worried about the chair coming with me when I stood up. When the maître d' told us our table was ready, I made a point of busying myself with my purse so he could get up without me noticing any struggle.

Once we got to our table, we ordered and our conversation turned back to the conservative conference.

"I'm so happy to finally have the opportunity to thank you for all you've done," he said.

"Oh, it's just my job. Did you attend the conference last year?"

"No, but I watched it all on C-SPAN. I'll definitely attend this year. Remember, I was the first one to register."

"Yes, I do remember." He had reminded me on more than one occasion. Sometimes I forgot that my job was other people's hobby. They didn't see the tedious tasks Thomas and I did every day. They saw the finished product. I didn't want to diminish their enthusiasm.

After dinner, we went to the hotel atrium for the inside snowfall and light show. As we navigated through the crowd, he put his hand on the small of my back. It was gentlemanly. After the show, we took the elevator back to my room so Preston could get his coat. We exchanged a few words while he stood there holding his coat.

"It was so nice to finally meet you!" I said.

"The privilege is all mine," he said.

He didn't make any moves toward the door, so I put my arms out to hug him. He looked somewhat startled. I'm not the hugging type, but it was the only way to end the awkwardness. After he left, I changed out of my dress and into pajamas. I went into the living room of my presidential suite and pressed the "All Off" button on the master light switch. I put the little cow on the nightstand and crawled into bed.

21

The new year had begun and I was determined to make it a better one. Christine and I made lists of three goals to accomplish in 2011. Mine were ambitious:

1. Lose fifty pounds.
2. Pay off Chase and Macy's credit cards.
3. Write a book outline and sample chapter.

Christine's, on the other hand, included the more personal goal of finding a boyfriend. On New Year's Eve, we put on funny hats and sat in my living room filling out our eHarmony profiles. We immediately got a few matches. I clicked "Send Questions" to two guys who had interesting profiles.

"You know, we're going to look like the biggest losers when some guy notices that we viewed their profiles at 10:30 p.m. on New Year's Eve," I said.

"Maybe they won't notice," Christine said.

"Yeah, maybe."

I would definitely notice.

"What's the deal with that guy you went to dinner with this week?" she asked.

"There's no deal, really. He's just a fan of the conference and wanted to meet me."

"But any potential?" she asked.

"I don't think so. It felt more like a business thing. I gave him a hug on his way out. Oh, he did give me one of those little Chick-fil-A cows."

"You never know what will happen."

The ball in Times Square dropped at midnight. We were in bed by 12:15 a.m.

Preston and I began texting a few times a day. Some of them verged on flirty. It was hard to read the situation. One minute he would be singing my praises, the next minute he would talk about me finding a boyfriend. Finally, I decided to be forward about it because it was just annoying. I had recently gotten similar e-mails from a preacher I knew. All of these conservative men were telling me they liked me in a roundabout way, but no one was making a move.

"Why don't you apply for the job?" I asked after another round of "you deserve a good man" texts.

"I don't think I'm qualified," he said. "You deserve better."

"What makes you say that?"

"You're an amazing person with an amazing job. I'm just a fan."

"You seem like a good guy. That's really all any girl wants."

"Can I tell you something?" he asked.

"Sure," I said.

"I was really surprised that you hugged me after our dinner. It meant a lot to me."

"Why wouldn't I hug you?"

"You're important and I've admired you from afar for so long."

"You admire me for my job," I said.

"No, I admire you for everything you are. Do you really think I would have spent a Saturday getting an online subscription to *Consumer Reports* so I could find a camera for you?"

I had forgotten about that. I just assumed he did a Google search for "cheap digital camera" and used his man abilities to know what the different model numbers meant.

"I really appreciated that. I bought the one you suggested," I told him.

"Maybe we can spend some time together at the conference," he suggested.

"I wish I could, but I'm always so busy. Maybe you could come by the night before it starts."

"I'll do whatever works for you," he said. "But there's something you should know."

Here it comes, I thought.

Preston then sent me text messages by the paragraph. I let him get out his entire story. He came from a well-to-do Delaware family. He went to Duke on a golf scholarship. (I didn't know such a thing was offered, especially at basketball-centric Duke.) He worked a full-time accounting job for several years. Then he developed an anxiety disorder. Things became harder for him. He gained weight. One night his anxiety got the best of him and the police were called.

"Who called the police?" I asked.

"My wife."

There it is. I didn't respond for a few minutes.

"Please don't cry," he wrote.

I wasn't crying, but I was disappointed. "Are you still married?" I asked.

"Yes, but it's not what you think," he wrote.

He then told me that they lived in separate houses. He told me that she knows about me and thinks I'm good for him. He described her as "Peppermint Patty."

"What do you mean? That she's a lesbian?" I asked.

"I know there have been meet-ups with women at hotels," he said.

"I think that makes her a lesbian," I said.

"We don't have sex. It's like we just have a business arrangement. She helps with my bills while I get back on my feet, and I help her with things in her life. Going to work events with her and things like that."

I didn't really know what to say. It was already late, and my sleeping pill was starting to kick in.

He continued, "The reason I didn't tell you anything before was because I didn't think you would ever talk to me like we have been."

He was being so sweet and I decided, perhaps under a diphenhydramine haze, that his story didn't change anything. We weren't dating, just talking. They lived apart, and she knew about me and didn't mind. Besides, he had one quality that outshined everything: he adored me.

The next week, the other staff and I checked into the hotel in preparation for the next conference. After orientation for the volunteers, I let Thomas and the other interns take them on the tour of the conference layout. We were expecting over ten thousand attendees, so our biggest concern was managing overflow. I went back to my room to work on the scripts for the master of ceremonies for each banquet. This used to be the job of one of the board members but had now fallen on me once I proved that I could do it. As the saying goes, the only reward for a job well done is more work.

Preston told me a few days earlier that he discovered he could use credit card points and stay at the hotel for the conference.

"I know you're really busy, but can I come by and say hi or bring you anything?" he asked.

"Actually, you can. If you're passing a Target or something on your way to the hotel, I really need some comfy slippers," I told him.

"I can do that. What size?" he said.

"I wear a seven, so it will probably equate to a small or medium, depending on the sizing."

"Anything else?" he asked.

"Nope, that's the only thing I forgot to bring."

"OK, I'll come by around eight. I don't want to take up too much of your time, and I'm meeting some other Duke alumni in the hotel bar for the basketball game."

"Eight is perfect. I'm on the tower side of the hotel. Room 8001."

I got to work on my computer, knocking out a few tasks and trying not to get sidetracked by the idiots who e-mailed me, the director of a conference of ten thousand people, asking for their booth number after I had e-mailed a list of booth numbers to them multiple times.

At precisely 8:00 p.m., there was a knock on my hotel door. I pictured Preston standing outside the door, looking at his watch and waiting until it was exactly eight before knocking.

I opened the door. "We have to stop meeting at hotel rooms like this," Preston said.

Yeah, he had that line in his head the entire day.

"I'm sorry this room isn't as nice as the first one," I said.

During the conference, my only room requirement was that it had a sitting area separate from the bedroom because people were always in and out of my room. I preferred that nineteen-year-old volunteers and the various speakers who needed a place to hang out before their speeches didn't see my dirty clothes.

"I like this one, too," Preston said.

He was so agreeable. "Here are your slippers. I hope they're OK," he said.

I untied the Kohl's bag and saw baby-pink slippers. They had thick soles and were exactly what I needed for shuffling from one side of my hotel room to the other after a long day of being on my feet.

"These are perfect! What do I owe you?" I said.

"Nothing. They're a gift for all you do."

Once again, I felt the need to fill the silence with a show of affection. I put my hand on his shoulder and gave him a peck on the lips. "Were you expecting that?" I asked.

"No, but I wouldn't mind more of it," he said.

He put his hand on my waist and kissed me. At first it was too much and too eager. I gradually got him to slow down. We made out for at least twenty minutes. It was nice, and I didn't want to go back to my computer. I knew there were hours of work ahead of me.

"I know you have a lot of work to do, and I should get to the restaurant for the game," Preston said.

"I do. I think I'm trying to avoid it at this point," I said.

I walked him to the hotel door. I kissed him again. Another ten minutes later we were still at the door. It was like all the stress of the conference went away when we made out. For a few minutes I didn't think about the millions of things I had to do.

Preston eventually left, and we made plans to get together again on Saturday after the conference ended. He also said he had a gift for me. He said it was a combination thank you/Valentine's Day gift.

Saturday came and the conference was almost over. Since it was the day before Valentine's Day, one of my assistants left candy and a nice card on my bed. I tweeted a photo of it. During those long days, it was always the little things I appreciated. A cold Diet Coke. My own stash of Chick-fil-A nuggets. Shoes that didn't make me want to cut off my feet after sixteen hours.

I texted Preston to ask if we were still on for that night.

"I think I'm just going to go home," he wrote.

It was an odd response given his enthusiasm all weekend. He had sought out Christine and Thomas because he wanted to meet all the important people in my life. He had texted me throughout the conference about how much fun he was having and how much he was looking forward to our Saturday night plans.

"Is something wrong?" I asked.

"Yes. That photo. It just upset me knowing someone else was in your room," he wrote.

"He's gay and it's basically his job to make me happy this weekend."

"But I want to be the one to do that," he said.

I was starting to get annoyed. "A hundred people have been in and out of my room this weekend. This is work. It's like my office. I want to hang out with you tonight. If you want to leave anyway, that's fine," I wrote.

"I do want to come. I was just upset."

Seriously, how do men deal with women and all of their insecurities?

After the conference closed and we had our party to thank the volunteers, I went back to my hotel room. It was over and I could finally relax. Preston would be coming at any moment. The hotel staff left me a tray of chocolate-covered strawberries to celebrate the end of the conference, so I snacked on that even though I planned for us to order room service.

Preston arrived (on time, of course) with a small duffel bag. We hadn't talked about it, but it was understood that he would be staying the night. I kissed him hello. He was barely in the door when my cell phone rang. It was Simon.

For several years I harbored an unrequited crush on Simon. Now that he had a steady girlfriend and it was fairly obvious he didn't like me in that way, I still considered him a friend and confidant. It didn't hurt that his mother was on my employer's board of directors.

"How you doing, LD?" he said.

"Good. Just getting ready to change into my pajamas," I said. I looked over at Preston. He looked ready to pounce. He started kissing my neck and rubbing my arms and legs.

Simon was talking. "My mom said there will be some big changes. I don't know what it means, but I wanted to warn you."

"What does that mean?" I asked Simon.

Preston continued touching me. "Can you just stop for a minute?" I snapped at Preston as I moved to the other side of the couch.

Simon didn't have any answers but told me his mother and the outgoing chairman would be watching out for me. I didn't believe him, but I didn't have the energy to think about that now. We hung up. A wounded Preston had left the sitting room and was sitting on the edge of the bed watching Fox News.

"Well, who knows if I'll still have a job after next week," I said.

"Why is that? The conference was a hit. They're still showing it on Fox News," he said.

"It has nothing to do with success. It's all politics. A new guy is in, and he's listening to all of these assholes who say having the conservative gay group hurt the conference."

"That's not right."

"I know it's not right. But that's the way things are. I don't want to think about it anymore. Let's watch a movie or something."

I changed into yoga pants. Preston offered up his lucky Duke sweatshirt. "Are you sure I won't change your luck?" I asked.

"Nope, you can only make it better. I want you to have it," he said, smiling. He always had the same crooked smile of a boy waiting for his mother's praise.

We stretched out on the bed and settled on *Saturday Night Live*. While in bed in Preston's sweatshirt, I watched *SNL*'s "Weekend Update" make fun of the crazy people at the conference. If they only knew the whole crazy truth, we would probably get the opening sketch.

22

The next morning, Preston and I woke up at around 8:00 a.m. It was my first night of more than four hours of sleep in weeks. Given that it was only our second (and a half) meeting in person and that I was completely exhausted, it was a PG-rated night.

"I wish I could wake up next to you every morning," Preston said.

"I wish I didn't have to wake up," I said.

"If you're awake, you'll get your Valentine's Day gift,"

"You've convinced me," I said. "Let me just take a quick shower."

I liked Preston but I was dying for some alone time, even if I had to settle for fifteen minutes in the shower. It was more a function of a long couple of months than him. After I got out of the shower, I sat with Preston on the couch for my Valentine's Day gift. I had told my friends Liz and Christine about the hints he had given me ahead of time, that it cost a couple hundred dollars and that it was something I could use during the conference. The consensus was an iPad. I was secretly hoping for something else. Unlike him and the rest of DC, I wasn't an Applephile.

"This is just something as a thank-you for the conference," Preston said as he handed me a card.

OK, so not an iPad. I opened the card and inside was a gift certificate for $300 of services at the spa at the resort where we had our first dinner. I was touched. A day of massage, facial, and mani-pedi was definitely something I needed after the conference.

"Thank you so much!" I said. I kissed him and gave him a hug.

"Of course, there will also be flowers because that's a given on Valentine's Day," he said.

"You are too sweet," I said.

We had plans to go out for a Valentine's Day dinner at Rosa Mexicano, my favorite Mexican restaurant, the next night. Having someone in my life who wanted to spoil me was exhilarating. Every kind word or bouquet of flowers seemed to erase the awkwardness of his marital situation.

On Valentine's Day, Preston insisted on picking me up. When I got into his car, he pointed to a Best Buy bag. "I bought some CDs I thought you would like so we could listen on the way to Rosa."

"It's only twenty minutes away," I said.

"I know, but I wanted them anyway."

"Well, I guess this one," I said. I unwrapped the Fleetwood Mac CD and loaded it.

In passing, Preston mentioned that he was a Quaker. Knowing a little about Quakerism, I wondered if that fact had anything to do with his marriage. During dinner, I initiated one of the oddest conversations on Valentine's Day.

"Is Aubrey also a Quaker?" I asked him.

"No, she's Lutheran," he said.

"Oh, I thought maybe you got married for religious reasons."

"No, I wouldn't have a Quaker wedding."

"What's different about it?"

"For starters, it's about the community. The bride and groom sit on a bench and are surrounded by the members of the church. They're all silent for a while. The elders decide whether or not to approve the marriage," he explained.

"So, they do this before the ceremony?"

"No, that is the ceremony. Instead of one priest or officiate, the entire church marries them."

"Do they ever say no?"

"They can."

"What would be an instance where they would say no?" I asked. "Like if they know the woman is a lesbian?" I was fascinated by these religious rituals that people just seem to do without question.

"No, not necessarily. Most Quakers actually support gay marriage."

"That's weird," I said. I (and the rest of the world) associated strict religious beliefs with fire, brimstone, and not allowing gays to marry.

"Then what would make them not allow a marriage?" I asked.

"Something that might lead to disownment, like if a spouse is too close of a relative. It doesn't happen that often," he said.

"Then why do they still do the ceremony that way?"

"It's just how things are."

That seemed to be the answer for a lot of things related to religion. Preston never talked about going to church, but he still seemed to respect the church's ways to some extent. Growing up with the religion probably fostered that. It's like an old, weird relative who still uses words like *mulatto*. Everyone knows it's wrong, but no one says anything because he's been around long enough to garner respect.

After Valentine's Day, Preston told me that I had inspired him to get healthy and lose weight. I always felt slightly uncomfortable when people told me that because I still had a long way to go in my own journey. But I still wanted to support him in any way I could.

"I've been paying for Medifast monthly deliveries for several months, so it's just been piling up. I'm going to start with that since I know it works," Preston told me.

"That's great," I said.

"I'm just going to take it day by day and week by week."

I remembered the time Preston told me he missed having a dog. I asked why he didn't get another one. He said it was because he wasn't physically able. I didn't know what he meant. Sure, a dog needed to be walked every day, but Preston could do that. He said it wasn't the walking, but if he slipped and fell or something, he might not be able to get up. I couldn't imagine what it must be like to feel that way. Even at my heaviest of well over three hundred pounds, I never felt like I wouldn't have been able to get up if I fell. Another time he told me he only wore slip-on shoes because it was hard to tie shoes. I liked that his slip-ons were at least Bruno Magli. He may have been bound to a certain kind of shoe, but at least he was bound in style.

"How about this," I said. "For every good week you have, I'll give you a reward. You don't need to tell me any numbers or anything. You know whether you're meeting your goal."

"What kind of rewards?" he asked.

"I'll think of some things and e-mail you a list."

After we hung up I put together a list of rewards. The greatest reward for him seemed to be spending time with me, so I focused on fun or cute ways to do that.

PRESTON'S REWARD LIST

1. Movie Night—Pick the movie and the place.
2. Board Game Night—Pick the game and the place.
3. Dinner at Casa de Lisa, dessert (optional)
4. Road Trip—Day trip to a nearby place, hand holding (optional)
5. Weekend at Casa de Lisa
6. A surprise gift (because I like giving surprise gifts)
7. TV Night—Couch cuddling and shows of your choice
8. A flirty voicemail message
9. Lisa's Choice
10. Dinner on Lisa (i.e., Lisa pays)

After the first week he picked a movie night. He had already seen *Black Swan* but wanted to see it again with me. It always seemed to take Preston a while to get used to me. It was like coming home to a puppy. At first he was excited or nervous; then he would eventually level off. Before the movie, he giddily told me about his favorite part.

"Don't ruin the movie for me," I teased. I didn't want to make him feel bad, but I also didn't want him talking throughout the movie. It was a major pet peeve of mine.

"I won't. I'm just so happy to be sharing it with you," he said.

I patted him on the knee as the lights went down and the previews started. When the lights came back on after the movie was over, I surprised to see that the ending had made him cry. I was reminded of when I saw *Passion of the Christ* with Joe the Catholic. I always seemed to be in a situation where I didn't match someone else's emotions.

After the movie, Preston and I went to a nearby café for a casual dinner.

"I keep thinking of the night we spent after the conference," he said.

"Yeah, it's always fun to get away," I replied.

"Maybe we can do that again. Go back to the resort where we had our first dinner. Have you spent your gift certificate yet?"

"That would be fun!"

When I got home, I checked out the rates at the resort. They were having a weekend special that included a credit at one of the restaurants. I sent him the link and he responded that it looked like a good deal and he would see about making a reservation.

A few days later, I came home from work and heard a strange noise as I was entering the first floor of my townhouse from the garage. I opened the door and saw that water was pouring out of the light fixtures. I could feel the water in the carpet squishing under my shoes. I ran up the stairs and saw more water pouring from the recessed lighting in the kitchen. There were pools of water on the hardwood floors. I raced up the stairs to the third floor to find the culprit. The carpet in my bedroom was soaked. I went into the master bathroom and heard the toilet running. I took off the tank lid and saw that the little floating bobber was stuck under the flap. I got it out of the way and finally heard the water stop running.

I went back downstairs. The water was still pouring out of the ceiling. I grabbed every bucket, trash can, and container I could find and started putting them under the places where the water was leaking. I figured that the toilet must have been running all day and water was in between the ceiling and floor and coming out in the only openings, the light fixtures.

After using every available towel to dry the hardwood floors, I called a plumber, then my mom and stepdad. They were just a few hours away in Williamsburg and would know what to do. Then I called Preston. I explained the situation to him. It bothered me that he had no expertise to offer. Some men try to fix things. Some men do fix things. And some men call other men to fix things. It was clear which one Preston was. At least he offered me his guest bedroom.

The next day I went to work while my mom and stepdad stayed to deal with water damage and wait for the restoration company. After work, I came home to fourteen jet engine–sized fans all over the house. The carpet and ceiling drywall were also gone. It sounded like a plane was landing in my house. They had to run twenty-four hours a day until the floorboards were dry. I thought it was going to be impossible to sleep with all the fans running, but the noise was tolerable when I went into the guest bedroom and shut the door. Thankfully, it would only be for a night or two, since Preston and I were going to National Harbor for the weekend.

On Thursday night I texted Preston. "What are the plans for the weekend?"

In the morning I was surprised to see that he hadn't texted me back. I texted him again. "Everything ok?"

Preston was usually texting me throughout the day, so to not hear from him for an entire day was unusual. By Saturday morning the message was clear. He was either dead or ignoring me. I finally got a text from him on Saturday night.

"Aubrey is staying here this weekend."

With that, I was done. I was OK with his unusual marriage situation because I was led to believe that it would not affect me. If she was still calling the shots and staying at his (OK, her) house, then I didn't want to get involved.

23

After the cancelled weekend, Preston's and my relationship, if it were one, fizzled to scattered texts over a few months. I texted him when I got fired. I was touched by his fervor when he said he wouldn't be donating or attending the conference because of it, but I knew they wouldn't notice. He asked if he could take me to dinner. I agreed. One shouldn't refuse a free meal when unemployed.

Preston offered to pick me up, but I suggested we just meet at a nearby restaurant. We settled on the only Chinese place I liked. They made an awesome chicken dish that used white meat chicken. Not this whatchamachicken most places used and covered in a sticky sweet sauce.

"It's good to see you," he said as we stood waiting for our table.

"You, too."

"I've lost thirty pounds since the last time I saw you," he said.

"That's awesome! I can definitely tell."

After we were seated at our table and had ordered, Preston asked me how I'd been.

"OK. Still looking for a job, but doing some writing gigs," I replied.

"I really wanted to reach out to you, but I knew you were mad that I didn't get you a hotel room that weekend," he said.

"That's not at all why I was mad," I said angrily. "I was mad because I was in a situation where my house was flooded and you said we were doing something that weekend. Then, rather than just tell me you couldn't, you ignored me for two days. It had nothing to do with the hotel, so you need to lose that.".

"Oh, OK. I'm sorry. I thought you were just mad that I didn't pay for the room."

"No, that was not it. It kind of makes me mad that you think that," I said. I didn't bother bringing up that it also bothered me that his schedule was dependent on his spouse.

"In that case, I feel even more special that you'll let me take you out again."

I softened. "Why not? You're a friend, and it's good to see you and see your progress."

After dinner we hugged, said good-bye, and went to our cars. I always hear about girls who dump nice guys because they've never been treated well and aren't used to it. I certainly didn't fall into that category. I took to Preston's fawning treatment like a duck to water.

The next day I received a beautiful flower arrangement from him with a note that simply said, "Thanks for seeing me."

I texted Preston to thank him for the lovely flowers. Judging by the small arrangements I sent to my sister and girlfriends on their birthdays, I figured this arrangement must have cost at least $200.

"Let's do it again soon," I wrote to Preston.

"Any time. While you're unemployed I want to be able to take you out whenever you're willing. It's the least I can do," he wrote.

Preston and I continued to meet for dinner every few weeks. He also continued to send me flowers with notes like "Just Because." When we went to dinner on his birthday, he insisted on giving me a $200 Target gift card. I gave him a historical novel by Bill O'Reilly. I wasn't uncomfortable receiving gifts because I knew he didn't expect anything in return. The Quaker value of equality didn't extend to dinner tabs. When we went out on my birthday, he gave me another gift card for my favorite spa. He also sent me two flower arrangements. One of them was my favorite flowers—peonies—in November. In November!

Preston was supportive during a time of depression and unemployment. During one dinner, he insisted on helping any way he could.

"I think Sidwell Friends is hiring," he said.

"The preppy private school?" I asked.

"It's a Quaker school. Like all the Friends schools. Maybe it would mean something if I recommended you because I'm an alum."

"Maybe. If they have an opening that would be a good fit for me."

The glee that came from Preston's flowers and gifts was short-lived. Not because of guilt, but because it didn't represent anything real. A few months later, Preston took me out to dinner for my birthday. It was good to see him doing well, though he was still married and being supported by his wife. He reminisced about our time together, as brief as it was. He expressed an interest in seeing me on a regular basis when he came to DC for conferences once a month or so.

"I know you and your wife have a different kind of arrangement, but since you've taken vows with someone else, that means something to me. The only relationship I can give you is one as friends," I said.

At the end of the day, Preston could only be a friend.

RYAN

the Preacher

24

Ryan was well known by college conservatives. He was a popular speaker on college campuses, and his books lampooning campus culture struck a chord with them. I first met him in 2003 when he spoke at an event I organized for summer interns in DC. He was in his forties and married but had quite a following among college females. I think part of it was his gun-loving, macho demeanor. He often spoke about the lack of masculinity in today's culture and the damage feminists had done to relationships. For conservative women like me who wanted a traditional marriage and not a man who thought of me as just a second income, it was refreshing.

I wasn't religious, but I respected Ryan's sermons. I read them online often and found myself agreeing with the sentiment, if not the doctrine.

Once I moved on from the women's organization to the conference, I brought him into the fray as a speaker on a panel. He spoke on a panel with other religious leaders who were more well known by the old guard. He raised some eyebrows when he came on stage to thunderous applause from the thousand or so students in the audience.

There was no doubt I was drawn to him. I was surprised and maybe a little excited when I heard Ryan was no longer married. It didn't take much to get the fantasy going. A few months after he spoke at the conference, I realized I hadn't sent a photo of him at the podium. "You hate me," I said.

"Not even close," he replied.

Around the same time, I noticed there was a little bit more of an edge to his e-mails. I also noticed that the public preacher was a bit different in private. I was used to Ryan posting about some of his female parishioners who attended services in inappropriate attire. One Saturday he went on a rant on Twitter about women with tattoos. Feeling cheeky, I replied that I had a tattoo.

A few seconds later he instant messaged, "Do you really?"

"You'll have to come to the conference to find out!" I replied.

"I sure will. I have a friend with a rifle tattooed on his back. So funny."

"My tattoo is the Republican elephant. It's on my shoulder, so it's never seen."

"You just got even hotter."

"Ha! I need all the help I can get."

"You underestimate yourself, Lisa."

"Oh, I'm just being silly. I know I'm awesome and any man would be lucky to have me. Do you know one?"

Then, realizing I might be setting myself up for rejection, I quickly sent another message. "Oh, you should do my interview column. I'll e-mail you the questions now."

I was fortunate to have a job that gave me favors I could dole out when I didn't think I was enough. I could give out speaking slots, better booth space, and personal promotion in a weekly column I wrote. I knew just me wasn't enough in a friendship, a romantic relationship, or a professional relationship.

I was surprised that Ryan didn't pounce on the interview offer.

He wrote, "Hmm, what are your requirements? (of the man, not the interview)."

I figured I had nothing to lose, so I was honest and didn't worry about scaring him away. He seemed so unattainable it didn't matter. I sent him my list.

Just off the top of my head . . .

1. Must like to get sweaty

2. Must not work "on the Hill"

3. Must laugh at my jokes

4. Must be taller than me

5. Must own guns (weeds out metrosexuals)

6. Must want kids and be ok with me staying home with them

7. Must have a life outside politics

"How tall are you?" he asked.

"5'5," I responded.

OK, I was probably closer to five four . . . or three . . . but what successful online relationship didn't begin with at least one person lying about their stats?

"I need a clarification on #1," he wrote.

"Yard work, working out, um, etc. All good things that make guys sweaty and more attractive. It's science!"

Was I being suggestive? Obviously. I had such insecurity with men being attracted to me, I felt like I had to say something suggestive to gauge his interest.

He quickly wrote back, "So, what do you like to drink—beer, wine, or the hard stuff?"

"Crown and ginger ale," I replied. Then I hastily added, "Very important addition to the list: Must love football."

"Football? Oh well, looks like I just fell out of the running," he wrote.

Damn it! Why did I just put on the "sassy sports girl" act? I hate that girl. And I'm not her. I remembered that Chris the Atheist got me into the NFL. Sundays were the only days we almost always spent together. I would cook for him while we flipped between games. (Oh, and add cooking to the list of things I do because just being me isn't enough.)

I wasn't ready to let Ryan the Preacher off the hook just yet. Certainly not just because of football.

"For you I would make an exception. As long as you are a fan of some kind of sport," I wrote.

"Baseball. But I drink beer, not the hard stuff. I wouldn't dream of asking you to make two exceptions."

Of course. He couldn't get out of this faux deal fast enough. I persevered.

"But why must we drink the same things? Is that your requirement?" I asked.

"I think we have reached an agreement. Save me a spot at the bar at the conference," he wrote.

25

It was September 2010. I already had four conferences under my belt. Professionally, I was on a high, but personally nothing had really changed. I was starting to be more vocal with Christian friends about my lack of beliefs and seeking advice on reading material. At first I was hesitant to ask Ryan for advice. I was sure he wanted any potential mate to be a Christian. Did I risk outing myself as a nonbeliever just to have a reason to e-mail him? Yes. I couldn't help myself. He often preached about men taking charge as the moral arbiter, so I figured maybe it wouldn't be a total turnoff. I e-mailed him.

> Is your new book about politics or religion or both? I'm really interested in religious conversations with people I respect. It's not that I'm an atheist, I'm just lost. For the last few years I've tried to find a religious path, but it's not connecting. I feel like it's a club that I'm not allowed to join!

He responded, "The book will be politics and religion. The club is open to everyone. Have you read much in the area of theology?"

Ugh, theology. I was trying to find a connection with God, not convince myself with doctrine. The next day I e-mailed him back.

> No, not really. Eric Metaxas gave me one of his books, but I haven't read it yet. It's "Everything You Wanted to Know About God (But Were Afraid to Ask)." I've listened to a couple of Tim Keller and John Yates sermons, if those names mean anything to you. I'm not hung up on

"why do bad things happen to good people," but I feel like the questions I have are juvenile for those who are already there.

He replied, "That is a short book. You should read it and if you have any questions, ask him. Then tell me what you thought of the book. I've been lost before. No one who was ever lost found his way without first taking a step."

I realized that I didn't really know much about his conversion. Perhaps I should read those books I was always raving about when selling him as a speaker.

Several days later, I gave Ryan a playful update on my progress.

"Woo hoo, reading sex in Metaxas's book!"

"Do you mean six," he replied.

"Both! six is on sex. Is this example of divine providence?"

Not surprisingly, he wasn't impressed with my jokes about Christian doctrine. "Beginning to think a book is not going to work for me," I said.

"The book is just the beginning. Visiting churches. Conversations. Lots of fun work to do," he said.

Ryan was starting to remind me of John the Evangelical. I had just begun having similar conversations with him. Why did these evangelicals think reading about how sinful we are was so fun?

Later that evening, I went back and read a few of Ryan's recent sermons. They were supposedly based in doctrine, but the practical advice, particularly on dating, just seemed like common sense.

"I read over a few of your sermons on dating. It's so frustrating to see so many conservative women behaving this way. Conservative boys certainly don't mind it either. One of the many reasons I'm totally over DC," I wrote.

"I was SHOCKED after my divorce at the proclivities of the first two 'conservative' girls I dated. False advertising, to say the least."

Ha! Now I had confirmation. He was no longer married.

"The stories I could tell you about the conference. That's why I enjoyed the sex in Metaxas's book. Many conservative girls are bent on proving that they're not prudes, and conservative boys are bent on proving that they're not the geeks they were in high school/college. I think these yankee boys are even worse," I replied.

Was I the opposite? I seemed hell-bent (heaven-bent?) on proving I could be a Christian. In the back of my mind, I remembered when I playfully ribbed Ryan for tweeting affectionately about a pretty woman. He wrote back that he was only kidding because she was an atheist.

"Any suggestions for my next theology book?" I asked.

"In the mood for something heavy or light?" he asked.

"How about one of each? Your light is probably my heavy."

He sent a list of three:

Light: *More Than a Carpenter,* by Josh McDowell

Medium: *I Don't Have Enough Faith to be an Atheist,* by Geisler and Turek

Heavy: *Mere Christianity,* by CS Lewis

How's that?

"I feel like Goldilocks. Thank you!" I wrote.

I was interested in how close Ryan and John were in their beliefs. Since neither seemed particularly interested in competing for my heart, I wondered if they would compete for my soul. I asked Ryan, "A few months ago someone told me that if a person has never surrendered himself to another person, it's harder for him to know how to surrender himself to God. Do you think that's true?"

"Absolutely not. Did that person have a Biblical basis for the claim?" he said.

"He didn't say."

"There are three keys to spiritual rebirth. I'll address them in my next three sermons."

Several weeks later, after reading the transcript of his first sermon on his conversion, I wrote to him.

"Many conversion stories start from rock bottom. What if you're just ambling along, living a mediocre life? How many books do I have to read before I actually feel something? Of course I know that it doesn't come from books. I'm just frustrated."

"Stay tuned," he wrote back.

I began to see a distinct difference between Ryan and John when it came to my salvation. John was more personal and took pleasure in bringing me into the club. Ryan seemed more interested in making sure everyone followed the club rules before they were allowed in. And I was just another pledge.

As the end of year grew near, I gave Ryan an update on my progress.

Hey there,

I just wanted to let you know that I appreciate your spiritual "guidance" over the last several months. I'm continuing this journey because of people like you. One thing it has taught me is that it may be time to get out of politics. New Year, new pursuits!

Best, Lisa

He responded, "Hey, how funny is the timing. I wanted to ask how things were going."

I wrote back:

Slow. I said to a friend that finding God seems to be a slow process for me. He said, "The good news is that God has already found you." I just wish I could connect to the words. Oddly, it's connecting on an intellectual level, but not on an emotional level.

I'm really turned off by those who wave the religious banner for the purpose of preserving political power. I won't elaborate, but that is also related to why I may leave politics altogether.

"The pace is unimportant so long as you are headed in the right direction," he answered.

26

The conference was less than a month away. The DC-based media was focused on the inclusion of a gay conservative group and the social conservatives who were "boycotting" the conference. Never mind that most of them had never participated in the conference prior to the controversy.

Around the same time, Ryan started to ramp up his sermons about the "homosexual agenda." Since I had strongly recommended him as a speaker at the conference, I began to worry about whether he would use it as a venue to criticize the conference.

"You're not going to cause me trouble are you?" I wrote.

"Can I make at least one wisecrack during my speech?" he said.

"Of course, I wouldn't have invited you otherwise. I just don't want a 'I condemn this conference' moment. The schedule reflects our principles. If other groups want to come in, that's great. But they're coming in to OUR tent, not pulling us out."

"I'm just gonna make a joke about how John Edwards joined GOProud."

"That's not even funny though."

"How about if I just call them a bunch of faggots?"

"It's been done."

"Can I say that the Packers reward for winning the Super Bowl was a booth at the conference?"

"You bring up gay sex more than the gays," I said.

"Stop it!" he wrote.

"Is it appropriate to insist on confirming all jokes with me before speaking on the free speech panel?"

"No, these are all fake ones," he assured me.

"Oh, good. I was afraid that you were only funny in books."

"You godless lesbian!"

"If I told you I could prove otherwise, I wouldn't be a conservative," I teased.

"Oh, stop it!" he wrote, I assumed in a stereotypical gay voice.

By the time the next conference rolled around, I was too busy to be nervous about seeing Ryan. Even though he told me to save a seat for him at the bar, the reality was I never had time to sit down during the conference for a drink. He was scheduled to speak on a panel on the last day. As usual, I was running around all day and tasked Christine with reminding me to be backstage before his panel.

My phone buzzed. The text said, "It's noon."

I was by the stage, so I made my way back to the green room. Ryan was lined up with the other panelists.

"There she is," he said with a smile.

"Hi there!" I said.

He reached his arm out and I gave him a half hug. We chitchatted for a few minutes. I told him the details of the panel, not realizing that the other panelists probably wanted the same information, but I was totally focused on Ryan.

"Well, I'm sure it will go well. I have to go back to the stage," I said.

"Yes, I'll see you afterwards."

I was on a post-Ryan high. At that moment, the lead-in speaker for the panel was coming off the stage. I patted him on the shoulder and said, "Great speech!"

He gave me a quizzical look and just said, "Thanks."

A few days later, I found out he had used his speaking time to lambast the conference for some reason or another. Well, that explained the look.

After the panel was over, I caught up with Ryan in front of the speaker lounge. Floyd was standing with him when I walked over.

"How did it go?" I asked.

"Oh, it was so much fun. I love this crowd," he said.

"Well, if you want lunch, we have Chick-fil-A in the volunteer break room," I said.

"I love those little chicken sandwiches," Floyd said.

Be quiet, Floyd, I thought. I looked at him and tried to will him to leave so I could talk to Ryan alone. Instead, I stood there while they both jockeyed for my attention. At times they talked over one another. Someone said something about carrying a gun in DC. Another said something about chicken. But, the conference being the animal that it was, I couldn't stand in one spot for more than a few minutes before a buzzing phone or person with a clipboard sidled up next to me with a request or question.

Floyd turned to Ryan and said, "Someone is always after her."

I could feel my face getting red. "OK, well, y'all go get something to eat in the volunteer lounge and I'll be there in a few minutes."

I was in my office just past the volunteer lounge when Christine texted, "Ryan is back here now! You better come back before he leaves! There are other girls here!!!!"

I loved that she was possessive on my behalf. I reluctantly printed yet another copy of the updated conference schedule and headed over to the volunteer lounge. I walked in and saw Ryan sitting at one of the tables, leaning back in his chair, sandwich in hand and surrounded by several of our college-aged volunteers. They all seemed to be talking at once. One asked for a photo with him.

"I'm glad you found lunch," I said.

"Yes, thank you. I love this place," he replied.

"Well, I'll let you get back to your fan club," I said, smiling. "Glad you could make it to the conference."

He looked surprised. I don't think he was used to his fan girls being the first to walk away.

27

Just before my annual trek to Palm Beach, I e-mailed Ryan to let him know I would be driving down I-95, passing through Georgia, where he lived.

"I'm headed to Palm Beach. How far are you from 95?" I asked.

"About ninety miles."

"If you drive closer, I'll buy lunch," I offered.

The next day I was fired as director of the conference. I was reluctant to tell Ryan. Now that I couldn't get him a speaking slot, would he answer my e-mails?

"I rescind my offer to buy lunch. I was fired," I wrote.

"What's next?" he asked.

I kept getting this nonchalant response from people, and it was really getting on my nerves. My job and my identity were taken away. It deserved more than the same question one has while reading IKEA directions.

I didn't know what was next. I did know that Ryan held the same views on the "myth" of gay conservatives that contributed to me getting fired. At that point, the only item on my agenda was to get as far away from those people as possible.

I didn't talk to Ryan for almost six months. As I became more publicly aligned with GOProud, the last thing I expected was to hear from him.

It was the first conference since I had been fired. The week before, I had found a new job and felt the presence of God in my life. Still, I was sensitive to the way the conference dominated the social networks and cable news that week. That weekend, my friend Christine and I tried to tune out the DC chatter by spending Saturday at the spa and a girl's night at a hotel in Northern Virginia. Christine was a great friend to me—and to her other friends. That weekend, one of her friends from her previous job was experiencing boy troubles, so she and Christine met in the hotel bar for drinks. I was really looking forward to lounging in the hotel room after a long day so I stayed behind.

I made an effort to stay off Facebook and Twitter, except for posting one lone article by a friend about why gay conservatives should be welcomed into the movement. I was bored and brought up the Facebook app on my iPhone anyway. I was surprised to see that Ryan had left a public comment on the article I posted.

"She's wrong. Being gay isn't a conservative value," he wrote.

I rolled my eyes. I was in no mood to get into a political discussion, particularly the same discussion that got me fired and had half the people I used to work with thinking I might be a closeted lesbian. I decided to defuse the situation by privately messaging him.

"I'm allowed to be bitter. How else would I get out my frustrations?"

Then Ryan the Preacher responded, "Or just crawl in the sack with me for a couple of hours."

Pardon? For no reason whatsoever, I looked around the room, as if asking the world if they had just read what I read. I decided he was probably joking. I wrote back, "That would end the rumors about me. Do you promise to tell everyone?"

"Only if you're really good," he wrote back.

I had to see where this was going. "Is there a sermon on crawling in the sack with you that I missed?"

"I'll write one for you," he wrote.

"It would be mean for you to tease me. I've had a crush on you for at least ten years," I wrote.

"If you were here, I would give you what you've been thinking about when you're alone."

OK, this is definitely venturing into new territory. Was this really him? "I think your account has been hacked, Pastor Ryan."

"I'll hack your account!" he replied.

OK, maybe it was him. He did have a corny sense of humor.

"Well, for the record, you can show me around your church any time," I said.

"What else?"

"You want more?" I asked.

"Much more."

I couldn't believe what I was reading. Just then, Christine came in after commiserating with her friend in the hotel bar.

"You're not going to believe this," I said.

"What?" she asked.

"You know that preacher who spoke at the conference last year? Ryan?"

"Of course. You have a thing for him."

"Yes! He's sending some very interesting messages tonight. I feel like he's drunk or something and doesn't know what he's saying."

"That's weird. I brought you back dinner. Do you want to watch a movie?"

"Sure. There's probably something on one of the movie channels."

My phone buzzed. Another message from Ryan. "Where are you?"

"This seems very out of character for you," I responded. "Prove you haven't been hacked."

Christine and I settled on some chick flick on HBO and mixed ourselves some drinks. Vanilla vodka and Sprite. It was a naughty cream soda.

My phone buzzed again. "I know you have a tattoo," he wrote.

"Everyone knows that," I countered.

"You sent me a book for my birthday."

Just because I had established that it was him didn't mean he was serious or didn't have something up his sleeve. I was still leery. I also didn't want it to stop.

"OK, so when do I get my tour?" I wrote.

"After you earn it," he said.

I looked over at the other hotel bed. Christine had fallen asleep.

"Your place or mine?" I reasoned that if I only wrote cheesy clichés, I wouldn't embarrass myself if this was just an elaborate joke. Or maybe he was trying to prove that supporting the gays led to lower moral values. I hardly ever drink. Was this naughty cream soda making me paranoid?

"Wherever you feel most likely to let loose and be totally uninhibited," he answered.

I still wasn't ready to fall into the trap of taking him seriously. "Ha, but would you respect me?" I said.

"Probably more. What would you do that would put my respect of you in jeopardy?"

"More? I think I missed that sermon."

"I think a ten-year crush should be rewarded," he wrote.

I decided it was time to say what I was really thinking. "I feel like this is a trap to show I have loose morals. Did I mention I went to church last Sunday?" I wrote.

"Sorry. It's not a trap," he quickly wrote back.

I was still hesitant but also very curious. "In that case, please proceed," I said.

"First an apology. Back injury this week. I am on pain medication. But I also have a very strong desire for you that is coming out. I just can't help it," he wrote.

"No apology necessary. You can't blame a girl for being suspicious."

"I think you would be really good in bed, by the way."

Was this really happening right now? I was enjoying the conversation because it was so out of character for him.

"Tell me what you want when we're alone," he said.

I was never any good at sex talk. Usually guys are so into what they're saying (or doing) that a well-placed "I like that" or "That sounds good" is all that's necessary. I had a feeling that wouldn't be enough for someone like Ryan. His entire livelihood was based on words. Words that comfort people. Words that save souls. Words that control people's behavior.

"Now you're making me shy," I wrote. How could I say anything remotely sexual when I had seen sermon after sermon where he talked about women acting like ladies and protecting their sexuality? I didn't know if my hesitation was because I wasn't comfortable talking this way or because I didn't know what he wanted and I was afraid of saying the wrong thing.

"Don't be shy. Tell me what you want."

Despite his desire to keep ratcheting up the sex talk, I was still afraid to act like I was into it. When I was head of the conference,my greatest asset was what I could do to raise his profile. Now that was gone, and I didn't know what to say to protect myself from what surely was an inevitable "sting"—on my morals or my heart.

"So you say. What happens when the meds wear off?" I wrote.

If I couldn't be sexy, I'd be coy. It was working, but I wasn't sure I wanted it to. I looked over at Christine. She was still asleep. What would she think of all this? Could she hear the phone buzz every time a new message came through?

I was embarrassed and lonely, and I didn't want Ryan to stop telling me the things I had been longing to hear from a man. All I wanted was to be wanted. Chris the Atheist didn't want me. Joe the Catholic chose someone else. John the Evangelical seemed to care about my afterlife more than my earthly life. Was Ryan the Preacher the one who could pull me from the years of feeling unwanted? I had to find out.

"Are you at the conference this weekend?" I asked.

"No. Don't change the subject. Make me want you," he said.

"I'm just fishing to see whether you're in the area."

"Are you alone?" he asked.

"No. I'm in a hotel room with a girlfriend."

"That's too bad."

"Why?"

"I wish you were alone so we could have phone sex."

"I've never done that," I lied.

Had I listened to a guy talk dirty and get himself off? Of course. Did I ever fully participate? Never. Also? Gross.

"I also want to give you some orders," he said.

I was still convinced this was a test. Was this man who routinely preached against women showing cleavage in public really saying these things?

"Remember, I'm a good girl that just had impure thoughts because of a ten-year crush," I told him. I also didn't want the conversation to end. "What would you tell me to do?" I added.

"I just want to tell you to undress down to your bra and panties."

"And?"

"I want to play with you. Will you play with yourself and tell me how it feels?"

Deflect, deflect, deflect, I told myself.

"I wish I were alone," I wrote. Just a gentle reminder that I wasn't alone.

"Is your friend asleep?" he asked.

I looked over. She seemed to be. "In and out," I said.

"I'll be in and out of you when we get alone."

"I knew you would say that. When will that be? "

"I don't know. I know I just need a release tonight."

"I wish I were with you right now."

"I'm going to go into the other room in a few minutes and make myself relieve this tension. Is your friend asleep?"

"Yes."

"Do you want to talk dirty to me?"

"On the phone, yes. But I can't tonight. She's literally three feet away from me."

"Step into the bathroom."

Well, he sure had all the answers. It wasn't like I was staying in the presidential suite. If my friend was three feet away, the bathroom was six feet away.

"You're going to get me in trouble," I told him.

His next message was his phone number. Then he wrote, "I can't wait much longer."

At that point, it didn't matter if it was his reading list or his dirty requests. I wanted to please him.

"I'll pretend like I'm going to take a shower. The things I do for you . . ."

"It will be worth it," he said.

I looked over at Christine. She was still asleep. I quietly went into the bathroom with my phone, closing the door behind me. I turned on the shower. It seemed loud, but not loud enough that I wouldn't have to whisper. I clicked on Chris's number.

"Hey there," he answered.

"I still don't believe it's really you," I said.

"It's me. What are you up to?"

"Just trying to stay away from the conference. So, I spent the day at the spa, now at a hotel just outside DC with a friend."

"Who?" he asked.

"Christine."

"I know Christine."

"Then you know why I'm hesitant."

"Don't be. I didn't realize you had a southern accent."

"Well, I am from Florida. Also, I've been drinking, so it comes out more."

"I like it. What else comes out when you've been drinking?"

"I don't know. I don't drink that often," I said.

I could hear his voice getting lower and his breathing a little heavier. After several more minutes of talking along the lines of our earlier messages, he moaned into the phone as he "released his tension." As I heard him let go, I stared at myself in the bathroom vanity, searching for someone else to ask, "Did that really just happen?

He hung up pretty quickly after that. I shut off the shower, turned out all the lights in the hotel room, and crawled into bed. Christine was still asleep. Or at least she had the good sense to pretend to be.

28

The next day, Christine and I checked out of the hotel. We were getting massages; then I would make my way back home. Ryan messaged to call him when I got home. Presumably, he was no longer on pain pills and I was no longer drinking. Did he want me to call him so he could apologize for last night?

Later that night, Ryan e-mailed. "Are you alone tonight?"

"Yes, why do you ask?" I wrote back.

"I want you to call me when you're alone and ready to take some orders."

Obviously, there would be no apology. I didn't mind.

"I'm going grocery shopping first, but I'll be home around 7," I wrote.

I immediately realized I probably just ruined his fantasy talk with real life.

"Tell me when you're home alone."

Well, I applauded him for seeing past my "grocery store" slip, but I couldn't decide if his bluntness was a turnoff or not.

A few hours later, I e-mailed him. "I'm home. Alone."

He didn't respond for over an hour. I began to question myself. Was the talk all he was interested in? Did I go too far in thinking he wanted to talk again? Was he turned off because I was acting like I wanted it, too? Did I want it? I refreshed my e-mail again.

There he was.

"Take off your panties."

"OK," I replied.

"Call me when you start to moan. Don't say a word. I'll just listen."

So, how long should that be? I felt like George Constanza in the episode when he skips out on a job interview and goes to a hotel room with a woman he met on the train. Before going into the bathroom the woman says, "Make yourself comfortable," leaving George to neurotically wonder what that means. Get naked? Just sit on the bed?

I mean, what if I call and start moaning when he answers, but it's the wrong number? Or he says, "How's the religious reading going?"

OK, that last one probably wasn't going to happen. That ship sailed somewhere between "Do you want light reading?" and "I'm hard."

Still fully dressed (underwear and all), I called Ryan.

"Hi there," he answered.

So much for not saying a word and just listening. This was good, though. Maybe we could go back to having real conversations with just a little playful talk sprinkled in.

"I saw your latest sermon was just posted. The ones you do on hate mail to the church are always popular," I said.

"Yeah, they really like those."

"So, what are you doing now?" I asked.

"Just getting comfortable. Where are you?"

"I'm in the living room. In my big, leather chair."

"Are you naked?"

I rolled my eyes. Why do guys always picture women walking around their houses naked? Is that what men do? If so, I think I'll never sit on another person's couch again. "I'm just wearing a T-shirt," I said.

"Do you like when I give you orders?"

"Yes," I said.

And I really did. It was the only way I knew for sure that what I was doing or saying was what he wanted.

We talked for over an hour. He told me what to do. He told me to be louder. He made me feel wanted.

Over the next few months, our conversations were intermittent. I had no expectations of anything more than an outlet for him whenever he wanted it. When I was lonely—or, more accurately, wanted attention—I reached out.

After a night out with John in New York, it was clear that he and I were never going to be anything more than platonic friends. I had started the night out in a new dress that I thought showed off my weight loss, but later I felt betrayed by the mirror when I saw a photo we had taken that night. I was sitting, which was never flattering. The thin jersey fabric of my dress was pulled tight against my body and my torso looked so short and stumpy, like I had no waist at all.

That night when John walked me back to my room, I knew nothing would ever happen. If I'm being honest, by that point my attraction to John was waning. After he left, I changed into my pajamas and plugged my phone into the charger on the nightstand. It was late, after 1:00 a.m. I reached over to my phone and sent Ryan an e-mail.

"I wish you would help me fall asleep. I'm in NYC all by myself . . ."

He usually responded pretty quickly. After thirty minutes, I gave up on hearing from him and eventually fell asleep.

I didn't hear from Ryan for several months. I tried to engage him, sending a few article links on issues I thought would provoke a comment. When I saw that a friend had written a column years before on one of his recent sermons, I goaded him.

"Smarty pants," he replied.

"Someone has to keep your ego in check," I replied.

"You need a good spanking," he said.

"Why? Have I been bad?"

"Come to think of it, I think you need a good hard f**king."

Reading those words gave me relief. Even though many times I was nervous about the escalation—how long until I had to refuse to send photos or Skype or FaceTime or whatever—I felt relieved that I was still wanted. Knowing that I could provoke these words from him gave me a sense of control, even though I knew I had none.

"What do you need?" I wrote back.

After spending a few days in Tallahassee visiting my dad, I rented a car and drove down to Tampa for the Republican National Convention. I was excited about GOProud's party but dreading the possibility of running into someone from the conservative conference. A hurricane was passing by the area, which cut the convention by a day. Unfortunately, it wasn't the day of the conservative conference's lame cigar party. I knew I shouldn't care about anything they did after they fired me, but I couldn't help but root for their failure.

The night of the GOProud party I was wearing a black and white cocktail dress with the best accessory—pockets. And also a black leather bracelet studded with spikes and rhinestones. It was so popular on the red carpet that a few guests borrowed it for their photos.

After the party ended, we piled into our rental van and headed back to the hotel. Despite the fact that I hadn't had a drop to drink and was exhausted, I was feeling unsettled after an encounter at the party. It was a brief encounter that I had been looking forward to since I bought my plane ticket, and it was now over. I needed someone.

"I'm at the RNC and bored. Entertain me," I wrote to Ryan.

"What do you want me to do?" he wrote back.

"A song and dance?" I teased.

"Hey, sorry, I cannot dance. I'm in my boxers only."

"Can you sing? I'm trying to be good and not think about you being in your boxers."

Yeah, I was not trying to be good.

"Can I tell you a fantasy I have?" I continued.

"Call me with the details," he responded.

"Number?"

I always asked for his number. It was my way of signaling that I never saved it. If he didn't really care about me, at least I'd let him know that I cared even less.

As always, he quickly hung up after he was done. If we were keeping score on who cared less, he was always winning.

A few months later, I met up with Christine for lunch. She was now dating a guy named Jason. She had a knack for good-on-paper guys. Usually homeowners who were slightly nerdy. They went on dinner dates, spent the weekends together, and were usually coaxed into running errands for her, which included bringing flowers.

"I need to stop talking to Ryan," I told her

"I didn't know you were still doing that," she said

"Not often."

"You know he's tried this with a lot of girls."

"I know, I know."

"He tried with me and other girls at my last job."

This I didn't know. "How far did you go with him?" I asked.

"I shut it down," she replied, then added, "You don't have to feel bad that you went along with it."

I didn't feel bad for doing it. The only thing that made me feel bad was not being the only one.

She went on, "I mean, has he ever asked you out on a conventional date? Has he asked you to dinner?"

How do you answer a person who has no idea what it's like to live in a world where good-on-paper guys are not an option? But I tried.

"Christine, you just don't understand. The options that are available to you aren't available to me."

I could feel tears welling up in my eyes as I continued. "Going to dinner isn't an option for me. Guys are not lining up to ask me out. Guys with multiple cars and six-figure incomes might be available to you, but they're not available to me."

I could tell Christine was getting impatient with me and my pity party. She said, "If that's what you think, then you need to do something about it. If you thinking losing weight is the key, then that's what you need to do. You need to put your energy into something that's real."

I knew she was right about the weight, but I still wasn't convinced that the alternative for my situation with Ryan was a normal relationship with someone else. The alternative was nothing. No flirty texts. No phone calls. Nothing to look forward to at night. A girl like me doesn't have the luxury of saying no. Being the go-along girl is my appeal. Ryan was proof that even the good guys don't like to be told no.

29

Despite my internal protests, I was now dating a normal guy. Scratch that. I was dating a guy normally. I had talked to Ryan once or twice, but I didn't see any point in mentioning that I was dating someone. It's not like he and I were dating. I also didn't know anything about his personal life. In fact, I removed him from my Facebook newsfeed because I didn't want to know. Dating or crushes or meaningless phone sex was so easy before social media. Now, every act is classified as stalking or petty. Or self-preservation.

"Are you going to the Student Activism Fourth of July party?" Ryan wrote.

"The boat ride? No, I didn't get an invite this year," I answered.

"Neither am I. Getting in too late."

Interesting. It was his way of telling me he would be coming to DC. Once again, like George Constanza, I was left wondering what my reaction should be to this news. But, wait, why did I care? I was dating someone. Why did I still want attention from Ryan? He always seemed to know to reach out precisely after I had written him off. Except I really never wrote him off. From the moment I started thinking about religion and the men in my life, I thought I had the perfect ending. Ryan was supposed to be the hero of the story. Wasn't he supposed to be Mr. Righteous despite over a year of less than righteous behavior from both of us?

A few days later, I got another e-mail from Ryan. "Where are you?"

"Alexandria, Virginia," I replied.

"I need room service."

The truth was, I wasn't prepared for anything real with Ryan. Real can't compete with fantasy. It was 11:00 a.m. and I was on my way to my boyfriend's house for a day at the pool.

"If you just dial 0 they can usually connect you," I said.

"Can they send a brunette?" he asked.

"You can usually make a request, but there are no guarantees."

"I want you. Room 1780."

"I'll put in the request for you. How long are you going to be in your room?"

"I need a brunette here by noon. Can she make it and then go to lunch with me?"

I didn't think this was what Christine meant by him asking me out for dinner. I wanted to say yes, but I couldn't. It wasn't guilt that I was dating someone and thinking of Ryan. It wasn't my Christian beliefs telling me it was wrong to give myself to someone who didn't care about me. It was vanity or, specifically, my insecurities. My hair was pulled back and I had no makeup on. I was wearing my bathing suit and a cover-up. I also hadn't done the myriad of things girls do before they're intimate—no matter which "base"—with a guy.

I wrote back, "Unfortunately, that's impossible. All sane brunettes are already at the pool."

"That's too bad," he wrote.

"For you," I responded.

I did it. I had said no. Did it matter that it was for all the wrong reasons?

ADAM
the Jew

30

I had just started my new job and was still writing for various outlets, which in this day and age means promoting yourself (and others) on social media. Twitter's appeal is the ability to force people to be concise (if you're doing it correctly). Unlike real-life activism, Twitter also gained me male admirers. Adam was a reporter for a conservative newspaper. We had attended the same events for years, but I never met him. On Twitter, we flirted and messaged one another while he worked. We talked about everything. People who annoyed us, the conservative movement, and that guys never asked me out.

"I thought you wrote 'porno' instead of 'promo' in that last tweet," I wrote.

"I love that you thought that," he responded.

"I have the sense of humor of a 12-year-old boy," I said.

"Then you should have no problem finding dates."

"Ha. Nope. I never get asked out."

"I'd ask you out in a heartbeat if I were single."

"See, all the good ones are taken."

Several weeks later, the conservative movement was dealt a devastating blow when Andrew Breitbart suddenly died. I had seen him a few weeks earlier when an organization presented us both with awards for our contributions in helping bloggers. Obviously, his contribution to bloggers and the conservative movement in general far exceeded mine. Driving into work as I read the news on Twitter, it was impossible to believe it was true. I looked over at the bag on my passenger seat. For no apparent reason, I had decided to bring the blogger award to work that day so I could put it on my bookshelf.

It's odd that whenever we hear of a person's untimely death, among the first thoughts we have is *but I just saw him the other day!* Like somehow if we've seen them recently, they're OK. There are people who knew him better than I did, but the wonderful thing about Andrew was that everyone who met him thought of him as a friend. I looked at my recent text conversation with him. My last text said, "Do you have a few minutes to talk today?" His response was "Sure." He was available to everyone, and it would surely be hard now that he was available to no one.

A few days later, a hundred or so conservative activists and writers gathered in DC in an organization's conference room to share stories and memories of Andrew. I was talking to Joe, my Catholic ex-boyfriend, when I saw Adam across the room. I did an awkward wave.

"You know he likes you," Joe said.

"What? What are you talking about? Wait, shut up," I said as Adam approached us.

"Hi, I'm Adam. Nice to finally meet you," he said as he put out his hand. His formality was cute.

"Nice to meet you, too! I'm glad you were able to come," I said.

"Yeah, I figured I would know some people here and I wanted to meet you," he said.

"Well, I'm glad we finally got to meet," I said.

He walked away and I looked over at Joe, who smirked at me and said, "See, I told you."

"Yeah, right. You can't tell by that exchange," I said.

"I can tell because he's always asking me about you," he said.

"Oh, whatever."

I brushed it off, but I was really pretty excited. We had a nice rapport online. I was curious if things would stay that way now that we had met.

After the memorial, a few people walked to a nearby bar for a drink. I wasn't in the mood, so when two friends asked if I wanted to go outside while they had a smoke, I followed after them. As we were standing there on the sidewalk, a car with a couple people in it slowed down. The girl in the passenger seat rolled down the window and yelled, "Hey, it's Lisa from Twitter!" I gave my second awkward wave of the day.

After the light changed and they drove away, one of the guys exclaimed, "You're Twitter famous!"

"No, I think they must know me. It just happened too quickly for me to see who it was. I feel bad I didn't recognize them."

"No, Lisa, you're Twitter famous," he repeated.

I smiled. Then I wondered, was that why Adam wanted to meet me?

I was back in Palm Beach for a few weeks of vacation. Now that I was working full time, I splurged on flying down and renting a hot convertible. I was still talking to Adam, but intermittently.

"When are you back in town?" he asked in a text.

"I fly into DC on July 16," I replied.

"Why so long?"

"It's not that long. I'm only here for two weeks."

"That's a long time. I don't want to wait that long. What's your number?"

Wait? What is he waiting for?

A few minutes later he called me.

"I just had to hear your voice," Adam said.

"Why?"

"Just because."

"What are you doing?"

"You don't want to know."

"Sure, I do."

"Your voice is just so sexy," he said.

After we hung up, I wondered how we got to this point. Why did he call me? Why did he want to hear my voice when we had never talked on the phone before? As much as I loved being in Palm Beach, I was now anxious to get back to Virginia to figure him out.

I got into Reagan National Airport in the early afternoon. As soon as I landed, I checked Twitter to see if Adam was still in Alexandria covering the women's conference. He was. I saw that some friends at the conference were getting together at Rock It Grill for drinks afterward. I decided it was a safe place to invite Adam.

"Are you going to happy hour at Rock It?" I messaged him.

"I didn't know that was happening. I wasn't invited," he wrote back.

"Well, now I'm inviting you."

"See, this is what I mean about not being in their clique and knowing about these things."

I was starting to get annoyed. "Stop whining. I'm inviting you. You're in."

I found a parking spot right in front of Rock It Grill. I didn't want to be waiting for him but instead wanted to walk in after he was already there. I look better standing up than sitting down. I saw him come around the corner. He was wearing a pink button-up shirt and khakis. It had been several months since we first met in person. He was taller than I remembered. I surveyed myself in the mirror. I was wearing jeans and a teal-blue blouse that showed off my tan and covered my upper arms. And, if I'm being honest, made my chest look amazing.

Just before I was about to get out of the car, my phone buzzed. It was the organizer of the happy hour. They were now moving to a restaurant that was at least ten blocks away. It didn't matter to me, though. Adam was already here, and I hoped he wouldn't be disappointed that it was just going to be me.

I walked in and immediately saw him sitting at a row of tables with a reserved sign on the end.

"Why are you sitting here?" I said.

"Hello to you, too," he replied.

"Hello. There's a reserved sign. We can't sit here," I said. "Let's just go sit at the bar."

We found two seats at the bar. The bartender took our order. I got a Crown and ginger ale and he asked for a cider beer.

"So, how was the conference?" I asked Adam, turning to face him.

"It was exactly what I had been telling you was happening. I couldn't get any good interviews. People would ignore me and then go sit with someone to do some podcast I've never heard of."

"That's because they also do podcasts, so they act like they're more important."

"I don't get that."

"Who cares? If they don't get that your newspaper is more important than a podcast that no one listens to, then they're probably not important enough to interview," I said.

"Yeah, I know you're right. It just annoys me. I don't want to talk about it anymore. How was Florida?"

"It was good. Look how tan I am!" I said as I held out my arms to show him.

He smiled. "That's pretty tan. It still amazes me that you say no one ever asks you out."

"Trust me, it doesn't happen. I was just talking to Christine about it the other day."

"I can't believe you're friends with her."

"What? Why?" I asked.

"She's a bitch."

I was surprised by his strong reaction to her. I had forgotten they briefly worked together a few years ago.

"But if she were here, I guarantee a guy would go up to her before he would come up to me," I insisted.

"I wouldn't," he replied. "I wouldn't even notice her."

"That's because you're weird," I countered. "It's not like I'm saying some guys aren't interested in me. It's just that they don't want to date me."

"How can you say that?"

"Because I'm living it. Sure, they want to have sexy talk or maybe go further, but they don't want to actually date me."

I then told him about Ryan the Preacher. Thankfully, he hadn't heard of him. A perk of confiding in a Jew, I thought.

"You deserve better than him," he said.

"You can't say I deserve better when better isn't available to me," I said. Part of me knew that he would disagree and I really wanted to hear him say it.

He looked in my eyes for a several seconds, then said, "That's just not true. I don't like you saying things like that."

I looked away.

After we finished our drinks, I offered to pay. He didn't put up a fight, so I gave the bartender my credit card.

We walked out of the bar and I turned around and said, "I'm parked right here."

"I'm around the corner," he said.

"Well, thanks for coming out."

"Come on, give me a hug," he said as he came closer toward me.

He put his arms around me in a bear hug. I patted him on the back with one arm while my other remained by my side. I was a bad hugger. When I was a teenager, I remember my dad's second wife (it only lasted a few years) and her family all hugged the same. At least they hugged me the same. Our bodies barely touched and I got a few quick pats on the back. It made it seem like the hello and good-bye hugs were just a formality, like they had to hug the step-relative because it would be weird if they didn't. Now, years later, I was hugging the same way. Not because I didn't want to hug others, but because I thought others secretly didn't want to hug me.

It was Tuesday after I got back from Florida. I had spent the afternoon at the dentist having a cavity filled and a wisdom tooth pulled. As usual, I messaged with Adam that evening while I watched TV and he worked

"This has been such a horrible day," he wrote.

"What happened?" I asked.

"Just assignment stuff. What are you doing tonight?"

"Nothing. I went to the dentist, so I'll probably just watch *SportsCenter*."

"You watch *SportsCenter*? That's so cool."

"Not every night."

"Can I come over and talk? We can still watch *SportsCenter*."

"I don't know. I'm not feeling that good. I got a wisdom tooth pulled out."

Truthfully, I didn't know what he was asking for? Did he really just want to come over and watch *SportsCenter* and talk?

"OK, I won't bother you anymore," he wrote.

I hate saying no. After years of hearing it in some form or another from Chris, Simon, Joe, and John, I knew how much it hurt. I couldn't say no.

"No, come over. Maybe it will make us both feel better," I told him.

"Thanks, baby."

I gave him my address. Then the inner monologue started. How does one dress when they have company at 11:00 p.m. at night? My best bet was to play it casual.

"FYI, I'll probably be wearing pajamas since it will be late," I told him.

"Good. Wear something comfortable and soft," he replied.

SportsCenter had just started when I heard a knock at the door. Before answering, I quickly checked myself in the mirror. I had opted for white terry-cloth pajama pants and a baby-pink top with an empire waist. Hair cascading down, of course.

I answered the door. Coming straight from his office, he was dressed in khakis and a polo shirt with the newspaper's logo.

"Your place is huge," he said.

"Yeah, it's about the right size," I said.

"Is it just you here?"

"Yes, just me. It's three floors. I like to have room to spread out. So, *SportsCenter* is on, but they're talking about baseball."

"What's wrong with baseball?"

"I don't like it. It's boring."

He sat on the couch not facing the TV. "I'm so tired. It's been such an exhausting day."

"So, what's happening with work?"

"I'm just pissed they gave some of my assignments to another guy. Even the stuff in DC."

"How many assignments?" I asked.

"Two."

"That's not that many."

"I know, but it's like taking money out of my hand."

"You're just being a greedy Jew," I teased.

"You're being an anti-Semite," he said.

"How can you even care? When's the last time you went to a synagogue or whatever?"

He ignored my question and asked, "Why are you sitting way over there?"

I was sitting on the other side of the couch.

"It's so bright in here," he added. He got up and stepped on the floor switch of the lamp. I didn't bother telling him he could just turn it off with the light switch. He sat back on the couch right next to me.

"You can't really see *SportsCenter* from here," I said.

"I don't care. I just want to see you."

Then we kissed.

After he left, the house seemed especially quiet. The next day I went to turn on the light in the living room. After flipping the light switch, I remembered that he had turned off the lamp at the floor switch. I didn't turn it back on. I wanted the reminder that he had been here.

31

The salon where I got my bangs trimmed every two weeks was near Adam's office.

"Hey, I'll be in your area tonight if you want to say hi," I wrote.

"Yes, tell me when you're here and then we'll go find some place away from everyone," he wrote back.

After my haircut, I texted Adam that I was outside his building. I stood there, trying my best to look aloof.

"What are you doing out here?" he said as he walked toward me.

"I told you I was here!"

"Yeah, but I thought you'd be in your car."

"So, you want me to go get my car?"

"Yes, dumdum."

A few minutes later I pulled up in my car and he got in.

"Drive up to First, then take a left," he said.

I followed his directions as we chitchatted. "Pull up behind this car," he commanded.

I did and shut off the car. The in-dash GPS seemed to be lighting up the entire car. I tried to press the button to dim it but instead pressed the button tilting it open. "Whoops, that's the wrong thing," I said.

"Did you steal this car?" he asked, obviously amused by my flustered movements.

"No, I just pressed the wrong button," I said as I took off my seatbelt and turned to look at him. He grabbed my hand and started stroking my arm.

"Tell me something good that's happening in your life," he said.

"Something good? We're getting ready for our big party at the convention. You need to come."

"Can I bring other people from the paper?" he asked.

"Of course. Just e-mail me a list of names."

He reached over and touched my knee. "If you'll be there, I'll be there," he said.

We began kissing, only stopping when a family with three or four kids were getting into the car parked in front of us. When we resumed, I ran my hand through his hair, pulling his head back, our lips barely touching. "You are so sexy," he told me. I loved hearing him call me sexy. I loved when he called me baby. There was nowhere I wanted to be but inches from him and steaming up the windows in my car. Every time the interior filled with the light from a passing car, we paused. It only made our kissing more passionate when the car became dark again.

"Are we going to have another *SportsCenter* party soon?" I asked.

"Who cares about *SportsCenter*?" he said.

"I thought you liked it and wanted to come over to watch it."

"No, I just like you," he replied.

After I dropped him off a block away from the studio, I drove home. My pulse was still racing. I could still smell him in my car. I smelled my hands. They also smelled like him.

A few weeks after that night, I arrived in Tampa for GOProud's convention party. Adam and I had exchanged a few messages about doing interviews in the club. I was excited about seeing him and doing everything I could not to reveal it to anyone else.

"Our newspaper friends from DC are coming. They'll need a place to hook up with people for interviews," I said.

"That's fine. They can be near the VIP area since that's where most people will be hanging out anyway," said Jimmy, the executive director of GOProud.

"When should I tell them to arrive?"

"I don't know. Whenever," he said.

"I'll tell them to get there around nine since that's when we'll get there."

Our party took place at a club in Ybor City, just outside Tampa, called the Honey Pot. We were expecting nearly a thousand people, so we arrived early to check things out. It was odd being in a club with all the lights on. I wondered if it would live up to the glamorous, party atmosphere for which GOProud was known.

I was talking to one of the club's employees about credentials when Adam walked in. Every time I saw him, he seemed taller than I remembered.

"Hey, tell me where to go?" Adam asked.

"First, get a wristband, then I'll give you a quick tour," I told him.

I turned to the club employee and said, "Give him the purple one."

As he put the wristband on Adam, I said, "This one will let you go anywhere."

Adam followed me up the stairs. I babbled about the three levels, who was coming, and how many people we were expecting. I stopped on the second level and pointed out the Drag Room.

"The Drag Room?" he asked, raising his eyebrows.

"Yeah, it's where the drag queens get ready and stuff. Tonight it's just where I'm keeping my purse."

"Interesting. I better go meet the others guys from the paper," he said.

Since I wasn't the face of the organization but knew all our friends and supporters, I was stuck at the velvet ropes nearly the entire night giving the go-ahead on whether people could be allowed into the party. Around midnight, I messaged Adam to see where he was.

"We just left. Too loud for interviews," he answered.

"That sucks. I'm sorry."

"It's fine. Set up some interviews for tomorrow."

I felt totally deflated. I had purposely showed him the Drag Room because it was the only private area. But he didn't even seek me out to say good-bye. After the party ended, the staff and I drove back to the hotel. I was exhausted and unsettled.

After the convention, everyone in politics was busy with the impending election. For campaign staff, it meant long nights and junk food. For the media, it meant more demand for airtime from activists and candidates and more demand for high-profile interviews. It had been a month since I had seen Adam at the party.

The next time we got together, I knew to pick him up a block or so away from his building. When he got into the car, he immediately kissed me. Then he said, "Drive."

I parked in our usual place. "I haven't seen you in so long," he said.

We kissed and then he stopped. Our lips barely touching, he said, "Did you miss me?"

"Yes," I answered.

"Tell me you missed me," he asked.

"I missed you."

"I can't wait anymore."

"Me either," I said.

"I want to be with you," he said.

I knew being "with me" was a temporary term. There was never any talk of his girlfriend, except the one time when he said "if I were single." They seemed happy. Unlike other women I imagined who had been in affairs, I never heard any promises to leave the wife or girlfriend. I didn't care. Even if only temporary, I wanted to be with him, too.

"I would literally do anything you asked me to do," he said.

It was great to hear, even though I knew it wasn't true. We found a spot near the water. It was early October, so it was really cooling down at night.

"Let's go for a walk," he said.

We got out of the car. He grabbed my hand and we walked along the Potomac River. There was a wonderful breeze. I would have walked across the Woodrow Wilson Bridge to Maryland if he asked. We sat down on a park bench facing the water. When I was with him, the rest of the world seemed to disappear. As we kissed, I didn't even care that other couples were walking around us. Or maybe, like us, they weren't real couples. Just two people who didn't talk about the rules of real life or real relationships.

Adam worked at night. For us to be together, it had to be in the morning. It was Wednesday morning. I woke at 8:00 a.m., took a shower, and went through my normal routine. I did my hair, put on makeup, then put on a clean Victoria's Secret sleep shirt. Adam was to arrive at around 10:00 a.m. I left the front door unlocked and told him to come up to my bedroom. Maybe he thought we were playing "sexy stranger in the house." I was playing "waking up with someone by my side."

I heard the front door open. I closed my eyes. Not to fall asleep, but to dream about what this moment would be like every day. Then I heard him coming up the stairs. My bedroom door opened. I kept my eyes shut. He kissed me on the cheek. I opened my eyes and saw him staring down at me.

"Hey," I said.

"Hi, baby," he said.

He got undressed and got into bed next to me. It felt so good to have his entire body next to mine. He was now with me.

Later as we laid in bed, I continued to touch him. Touching his lips, his eyebrows. Everything, including everything.

"Your hands are angelic," he said.

I laughed. "Yes, this is what angels do."

"Then kill me now. Take that pillow and put it over my face. I'll go to heaven," he said.

"But you're a godless Jew," I playfully countered.

"Then I'll convert first."

"You'll accept Jesus?" I asked.

"Yes, I'll accept Jesus as my lord and savior."

After he left, I felt more lonely than ever before. I didn't even have time to feel remorseful or guilty. The house just felt more empty. It reminded me of a time when I went to the shooting range at night. After an hour of being empowered by practicing my marksmanship, I packed up the Glock 19 I borrowed from the range and then headed to the mall. As I walked back to my car in the dark, nearly empty parking lot, I was so much more aware of not having a gun to protect me. I had walked through parking lots at night hundreds of time. But after having protection and then going without it, I was more aware of what I was missing. Being with Adam now made me acutely aware of how lonely I was once he left.

I spent the rest of the day in my sleep shirt.

Adam and his girlfriend lived together. They shared a bed and three cats. On the weekends, I didn't expect anything from Adam. Of course, I didn't expect much from him during the day either. I was in a place where getting a notification that he was playing Words with Friends made my day. How did I get so wrapped up in a situation in which "Adam has made a move" was the highlight of my weekend?

Weekends are for wives. Even though I desperately wished there was something real between us, when it comes to men, Newton's third law of motion was correct: "An object at rest stays at rest and **an object in motion** stays in motion with the same speed and in the same direction unless acted upon by an unbalanced force."

A man living with a woman is an object at rest. I may have been unbalanced, but I wasn't a force.

One Sunday I tweeted about a good deal I found on daisy poms at Safeway. (Yes, Twitter can be mundane, but lately I prefer my fellow politicos' mundane tweets over their political ones.)

"I thought that said PORN daisies," Adam private messaged me.

"It's too late in the season for porn daisies!" I joked.

"I do like Safeway better than Giant," he wrote.

Um, OK. I was surprised by this random conversation on a Sunday.

"Me too. Testing recipes before Christmas. Today, Chocolate Peanut Butter Caramel Rice Krispies Bars. Not very fancy, so may not make the cut."

I knew Adam had a sweet tooth and might appreciate my efforts.

"It's October," he said.

So much for scoring points that way. "I know, but I want to try different things. I bring a new thing to work each week to get their opinion. Don't make fun of me."

"It's very generous," he said.

"Why aren't you playing Words with Friends with me?" I asked.

"WTF I just DMed you about it."

The previous day he had remarked that I was always beating him. This was not something I minded. No man was worth throwing a Words with Friends game.

"Don't WTF me," I told him.

"Just F you?"

"If you want," I said.

"Duh," he responded.

I was reminded of the times when Ryan the Preacher would start our phone calls with complaints about daily life. As much as I loved the mundane conversation with Adam, I needed that extra validation that he wanted me. Once I got it, I was relieved. I wouldn't respond so that the last word was his desire for me.

By Monday morning I needed another fix. Picking up on his last message, I wrote, "So give me details, smartypants."

"What is your schedule?" he asked.

"I can play hooky later in the week."

"Deal and deal," he said. Then he messaged a few second later, "Any play time in your car one night this week?"

Looking at my iPhone calendar, I decided Wednesday was the best day. It would give me time to go home and freshen up after work. Also, it was soon enough in the week to bring him the leftover Chocolate Peanut Butter Caramel Rice Krispies Bars.

"You just made my day. I can do Wednesday," I wrote.

"Sweet," he said.

"What time?" I asked.

"Sundown," he said.

"I need tinted windows."

"Or a van," he said.

"Or it would be better for you to miss me."

"Your ass better be in Arlington tomorrow night," he said.

"I like demanding Adam."

"The verb or the description?"

"I need to test the verb," I said.

"That just got me," he said.

I didn't respond.

The next day I was positively giddy about seeing Adam. Every hour at work seemed to drag by. When I was finally driving home from work, the excitement was almost too much. The thirty minutes we spent talking and making out in my car was the highlight of my week. Accidentally seeing photos of him and his girlfriend were erased from my head during those minutes when he was holding my hand. I had no animosity toward her. I didn't even want to be her. I just want a man who cared about me. A man who would spend the weekend taking me someplace fun or new.

Just as I turned into my neighborhood, I got an e-mail from Adam.

"We're on standby. Can't leave the office until guy I'm interviewing arrives. Can we do tomorrow instead?"

I wasn't mad at him. I was mad at myself. Mad for being excited about something that wasn't mine. I was so deflated that tomorrow seemed like never.

"I can't tomorrow until after 8 p.m., which is probably too late for you. Oh well, another time," I wrote.

"Better than nothing. I miss you. Come by tomorrow."

I didn't want to feel this way again. I didn't want to get my hopes up, and I felt silly that our brief encounters were so important to me. I also wanted validation that I wasn't the only one who felt this way. Like on my last day of school with the girls I thought were my best friends. Or my trip to New York with Joe the Catholic. I didn't want to be the one who was always oblivious to what was really going on.

I wrote back to Adam, "We'll see. Watching a friend's dogs. Depends on if I go home first."

After not receiving a response, I decided I couldn't take the possibility of one-sided excitement. "I don't think tomorrow will work. I miss you, too," I wrote back.

"Blame this guy who hasn't shown up yet," he wrote.

I didn't blame Adam and I didn't blame this mystery guy. I blamed myself for letting someone get to me. Especially someone who wasn't available. If you know a relationship is doomed or has an expiration date, a rational person wouldn't proceed. But I irrationally continued because those evenings of messages or twenty minutes of hand holding were all I had. When you're starving, you don't care about where your next meal will come from. You're only concerned about the meal in front of you right now, because the next one might never come.

In the play *The Women* by Clare Boothe Luce, Mrs. Morehead, the mother of a woman who suspects her husband is having an affair, tells her, "A man has only one escape from his old self: to see a different self in the mirror of some woman's eyes."

I have a knack for seeing the need in men. Most of the time it's not as the other woman, but the little things men need to hear. One evening I noticed Adam was tweeting several funny political observations. There wasn't much interaction from our common political friends, so I thought I'd give him a little boost. I retweeted one of them and sent him a DM.

"You're funny tonight."

"Wow, thanks," he wrote. "I was about to give up on Twitter. I can't get a single reaction, but you liking it means more than any stranger."

"I'll retweet you all night long," I joked.

"Thanks, love. You are awesome and brightened my crappy night."

"Aww, that makes me happy then. Why is your night crappy?"

"Just nothing working out lately and lots of crap going on here."

"Well, I'm glad I could brighten your day. Don't be down."

"Thank you, baby."

It was 10:27 p.m. I knew I would sleep well that night.

Adam came from the nonpolitical world and often got frustrated with the lack of respect he and his new newspaper received. After nearly fourteen years in the conservative movement, I had built a list of random contacts that seemed to have their hand in everything. Similar to when I cooked or baked for Chris the Atheist or interviewed Ryan the Preacher, I tried to help Adam whenever I could. I only felt confident when I could be useful.

When Adam was in Boston covering election night for the Romney/Ryan presidential campaign, he wasn't able to get into the main ballroom where political pundits were roaming and giving interviews.

He wrote, "I'm stuck in the media filing center. I can't get into the ballroom."

Coincidentally, John the Evangelical was there and close to the campaign. I texted him that Adam needed access. He said he would work on it.

I e-mailed Adam, "Just texted a friend with the campaign. Where are you sitting so he can find you?"

"What are you talking about? How did you even know it was an issue?" he wrote back.

"Because you just tweeted it."

"Press room, row U. But you said you had someone almost immediately after I complained. You're unreal. I'm literally sitting here dazed."

I knew he meant everything he was saying as a compliment, but it really annoyed me. We'd been talking nearly every (week)night and randomly seeing one another for several months now. Why was it so out of the realm of possibility that I would help him out? Wouldn't he do the same for me?

I was reminded of when I was cooking for Chris the Atheist. On our Sundays watching football, I would buy a pound or so of chicken breasts and other healthy food and spend a few hours cooking meals for him to eat for the week. When he tried to pay me for my efforts, I took it as an insult. I was behaving like a good girlfriend. The only payment I wanted was appreciation. Or acknowledgment that despite not being the prettiest or the skinniest, I was the best. I just wanted approval: you are good and I'm glad to have you around.

"I'm waiting to hear back from my guy. He might be too busy to get to you," I told Adam.

"Even if it doesn't work out, just that you tried. Wow," he wrote back.

Trying wasn't enough for me, though. I wanted to deliver. If I didn't, why would he want to keep me around?

32

Bridget Jones is my spirit animal. Not only do we have the same bad boy vs. good boy struggles, but we also have the same birthday. We're also looking for someone who likes us just as we are.

I often joked with friends that I didn't get asked on dates because I was on the board of directors of an organization for gays and their allies. Usually it was just to deflect the natural questions that came from well-meaning friends and relatives about why I was single. As Bridget Jones said, "Suppose it doesn't help that underneath our clothes our entire bodies are covered in scales."

And I suppose it didn't help that half of DC thought I was a lesbian. Of course, the pool of conservative lesbians comprises about four people, and they all know I'm not on their team. So, I don't even get the added ego boost of getting asked out by women.

One night I got a surprising e-mail from Adam.

"Holy crap, now I realize what you deal with. Another reporter JUST NOW: I know she plays for the other team, but I'm really into Lisa D. I set him straight. He said he looked you up online and found all that lesbian stuff," he wrote.

This was an interesting development. "Who said that?" I asked.

"No names. I don't want the competition," he wrote.

Given that he wasn't single and was in no position to make rules when he was breaking rules, I wasn't sure if I was angry or flattered.

"Is he funnier than you?" I asked.

"Yes, he's all yours. Nice knowing you."

"Wait, what do you mean by all that lesbian stuff?" I asked.

"He said he looked you up online and found something that called you a conservative lesbian."

"If you have any future inquires," I told him, "I'm straight."

"I told him that immediately."

One evening I was taking a bubble bath when I remembered that Adam had remarked that my bathtub was huge. I told him it was big enough for two. He wasn't so sure, so that evening I sent him a photo of the empty half of the bathtub.

"See, plenty of room," I wrote.

A few minutes later he responded, "Stay in. I'll be there after work."

I couldn't very well stay in the tub for the next three hours, so I got out and drained the tub. I dried off and freshened my makeup.

A few minutes later he asked for my address like he always did. I wondered if he was doing the same thing I used to do when I asked Ryan the Preacher for his phone number. Maybe it wasn't mind games but that we both had convinced ourselves that each time was the last time. Don't save the number or the address, because that would be like acknowledging we would see one another again.

I don't think Adam ever thought he was doing anything wrong. He was Jewish, but not religious. He was as publicly supportive of Israel as Ryan the Preacher was for abstinence. I began to feel guilty for my part in their bad behavior. Were they both good, but I was making them bad?

I shook the thought out of my head and turned on the faucet. Like before, Adam would let himself in and come up to the bedroom. I made sure the water was extra hot so it wouldn't be cold by the time he arrived. I squeezed the pink bubble bath into the water and watched it swirl.As the bubbles began to form, I dipped a toe in. The water was scorching hot. I sat on the edge of the tub while it filled up, figuring the hot water out of the faucet would cool down soon. When the tub was almost filled, I turned off the faucet and stuck both feet in. It was almost too hot to bear. I slowly slid down into the giant tub. My skin felt like it was being seared, but I endured it so the water would still be warm for him. And let's face it, cold water diffused bubbles, and I looked better covered in bubbles.

Before he arrived, I put on my usual bath-time playlist. First I checked to make sure there weren't any songs that would lead to awkward moments. "Call Your Girlfriend" by Robyn? Definitely a mood killer. But it was starting to grow on me over the last few months.

Call your girlfriend, it's time you had the talk.
Give your reasons, say it's not her fault
But you just met somebody new.
Don't you tell her how I give you something
That you never even knew you missed.
Don't you even try and explain
How it's so different when we kiss.

I pressed play and leaned back to finish reading a copy of *Lucky* magazine that was now as wrinkled as my fingers. It was almost 12:30 a.m. when I heard my bedroom door open. Adam opened the bathroom door. I looked up at him and smiled.

"You're killing me," he said.

He left the bathroom. I could hear him getting undressed in the bedroom. He came back in and eased himself into the opposite side of the bathtub. We were facing one another and the water was now almost to the edge so that every move pushed a little water out.

"Get closer to me," he said.

I tried to gracefully move around in the tub. It was clear that it was nearly impossible to stay under the water and not make those embarrassing noises of skin slipping on porcelain. In other words, I was trying to avoid something that sounded like a fart while he saw me completely naked. I managed to get my legs under me so I could lie down on his chest.

"How's that?" I asked.

"Perfect. This feels so good."

We were in the bathtub for several rounds of my bath-time playlist. We didn't talk much. I'd say something silly and he'd say "What, baby?" I think I may have been mumbling just to hear him say *baby*. After nearly three hours in the tub, we dried off and went to my bed. It was after 4:00 a.m. when he left.

Being with Adam was like going under an overpass during a rainstorm. For a split-second, the noise of the world disappears and there's just comfortable silence. It's jolting when you realize it's over, it's still raining, and the world still goes on.

I rationalized that it was OK to see Adam despite him having a girlfriend because there were no expectations. We were just two people who met a year too late. When I could feel myself get too close to him, I would withdraw. Around Christmas I decided to avoid Twitter for a few weeks. After two weeks off of Twitter, I saw that Adam had tweeted that one of the things he was thankful for in 2012 was meeting two random political tweeters and me. I was surprised given that we hadn't talked in a while. I sent a quick e-mail saying thanks.

He quickly messaged back, "Where in the hell have you been?"

I was flattered but also annoyed that the onus of contact always fell on me. I hated myself for pursuing him even though he was more than willing to pursue me, too.

After Christmas, I was walking in Arlington one evening when I saw Adam on the street. He was in the doorway of a large office building. He was kissing a girl with short, very blonde hair. I had seen his girlfriend in photos. She had long brown hair. He wasn't kissing his girlfriend. I hurriedly walked back to my car so he wouldn't see me. I only had one thought in my mind. Where there is one, there is many.

I wasn't angry at him. I was angry at myself for thinking I was special. Just like I thought I was with Ryan the Preacher. Somehow I thought that if I was behaving in a way contrary to what Christianity told me, it was OK because Ryan and Adam pursued me. They were the ones who were wrong.

I stopped messaging him in the evenings. He never asked why. A few months later he asked me for the URL of the job website I had told him about when he was complaining about his job. It was a subscription service that you had to pay for each month. I let him use my password for a little while but eventually canceled it. I suppose he realized that when he tried to sign in.

By March it was time for the conservative conference. I knew he would be covering it for his paper and decided to use it as a good reason to disconnect from him on Facebook and Twitter. Oddly, I had endured his posts with his girlfriend and even the banter I saw him have with the blonde (in between her tweets about her husband and kids), but I couldn't take the tweets praising the people who fired me.

Once again, Christine and I held an anti-conference happy hour. We had two other previous directors, my former assistant Thomas, Joe the Catholic, friends, and several media folks.. The mood was meant to be jovial and "we're too cool for that conference." Unfortunately, I had just found out that week that I would be losing my job. The organization was being acquired by another organization based in New York, and they had no need for a DC office. I just wanted to get through the party and the weekend of the conference without dwelling on the disappointment of losing another job.

Christine and I were headed to Atlantic City for the weekend. We splurged on pedicures, but I limited myself to only spending $40 on the slots. I decided not to worry about starting a job search—again—until I got back to Virginia.

Tuesday after we got back I e-mailed Adam.

"Hey, I'm losing my job. Can I use your password for that jobs website? Pretty please?"

A few minutes later he e-mailed me back the user name (his e-mail address) and the password. His password was my name. Every time he logged in, he was typing my name. Did I still mean something to him, or was it just to make me think I meant something? I couldn't let myself try to find out.

"Thanks," I wrote back.

A few weeks later Adam e-mailed, "How's the job search?"

"Aww, it's cute when you pretend to care," I wrote back.

"Shut it. I do."

"Well, I did get an offer, but I'm not sure if I should take it," I wrote. "It pays a little less and I'll have to give up all social media and writing income. I just feel like I shouldn't turn away a job."

"Don't do it. You're losing too much."

Everyone else was telling me to take the job, but I was dreading it. I knew it wasn't the right fit for me.

"You're the only one who told me what I wanted to hear. Now I'm crying."

"I am sorry, love. Please don't cry," he wrote.

I couldn't respond. I hated that he could still have an effect on me. I was so empty that I sucked it right up.

A few days later, I saw a mutual friend post a photo. Adam and his girlfriend got married.

Our e-mails became less frequent. I thought about him less and less. It helped that I had just started dating someone I met on a Christian dating site. I happen to see two of his coworkers at a bar in Arlington one night. They were both married and seem to live vicariously through me. I told him about the guy I was dating.

The next day I got an e-mail from Adam, "So. Boyfriend. Do tell."

That didn't take long. I wrote back, "Don't you hens have anything else to talk about?"

"Tell me about him," he wrote.

"I will later. I'm at the beach," I told him. I was watching a friend's dachshund (Auggie!), and I took him to Rehoboth Beach, Delaware, for the day. Unfortunately, dogs weren't allowed on the beach during the summer, so we were prancing down Rehoboth Avenue. He was small enough to carry into stores. I had just ducked into a store that sold signs my boyfriend's mother made when my phone buzzed again.

"Is your boyfriend with you?" Adam wrote.

"No, just here with Auggie for the day."

"Why not him?" he asked.

"He's at work. I wanted to come during the week when it wasn't as crowded. Also, I'm dogsitting and he's not a dog person."

"How can you be with a man who isn't a dog person?" he asked.

"It's not that he doesn't like dogs, but that he prefers cats," I answered.

"This will end soon," he said.

I rolled my eyes. Now Adam was an expert on relationship stability? We hadn't exchanged this many words in over six months.

"Did those hens at your office say anything else about him?" I asked.

"Just that your boyfriend is blind. Nothing else."

So, he did know that part. I sometimes hesitated to tell people. Not because I was embarrassed, but because it always led to a million other questions.

Adam was no exception. "Is your boyfriend really blind? Like totally or just legally?"

"Totally, since birth," I told him.

"What are you two doing tonight?"

"We're not doing anything tonight," I wrote back.

"Dump him if he's a cat person," Adam wrote.

That was rich coming from him. Trouble in paradise with his wife and their cats?

He e-mailed again. "It's fun goofing with you again."

Perhaps now he thought it was safe to talk to me because we were on an even playing field. We were both in relationships. "I'm bored and have time on my hands," I wrote.

"I'm glad I'm associated with boredom. What's your number?" he said.

"I'm poking fun at myself for being unemployed. Remember, if there's a jab it's almost always directed at me," I wrote back, along with my number.

I wasn't sure why he wanted my number. A few minutes later the phone rang.

"Hello?" I answered.

"So, tell me about the blind guy. I don't want to know his name. He's just going to be the blind guy," he said.

"What's to tell? We've been dating for two months."

"Have you had sex?"

"No, not yet. He's a good guy, unlike you."

"There must be something wrong with him then."

"Why? Because he's good?"

"No, because he's able to be around you and not have sex with you."

"I'm trying to be better," I told him. "Plus, he hasn't exactly brought it up."

"That's unreal. I can't even take listening to your voice right now."

I knew I should wrap up this call, but I wanted to see where it was going. It made me feel good that I had some sort of power over him. I immediately forgot about his wife, the blonde, and my boyfriend.

"What are you doing?" I asked.

"You know what I'm doing. Just keep talking."

So, I did. I talked about the time we were in the bathtub. I talked about an afternoon I spent with my boyfriend. I talked until he was finished. When we hung up, I didn't feel guilty or sorry. I was elated that I could still have an effect on him.

Over the months we didn't talk about the random phone call out of the blue. He didn't ask about "the blind guy." We made plans for lunch several times, but something always came up and he canceled. It made me wonder if he thought he couldn't trust himself around me. Maybe he had finally decided to be the good guy. Maybe he could live with himself if he cheated on his girlfriend, but not if he cheated on his wife.

Every once in a while I'd see him pop up in my Twitter feed because someone retweeted him. He was still trying too hard to be noticed. That's what I gave him. When he looked in my eyes, he saw a version of himself that was funny and sexy and wanted.

Sometimes his name came up in conversations with other conservatives, but not often. I was having drinks with a friend who was in town after one of the regional conservative conferences. I never heard much about the activists who attended them. Most of the attendees seemed to be conservative and liberal media, bloggers, and people who worked for other conservative organizations. Adam was usually there, still begging for interviews among the podcasters.

The regional conferences also breeded "conference only" hookups. My friend Samantha told me that Adam had been sending her inappropriate messages before the conference and she had refused to hang out with him alone. She told me she was thinking of filing a complaint with his newspaper. I told her he was probably just tired or drunk or both.

Then out of the blue, I saw Adam on the street. He was on the other side of the street, soI waved. He crossed the street to greet me. I had just left lunch with Joe the Catholic. He was sitting in the car as this awkward meeting played out in front of him.

"What are you doing here?" Adam asked.

"I just finished meeting a friend for lunch."

"How have you been?"

"Good. I got a book deal," I told him. "Still looking for a job, but I like having the time to write. Especially about things other than politics."

"I hear that," he said.

I looked at his left hand and noticed he wasn't wearing a wedding ring. I smiled at him. Even though I didn't follow Adam on Twitter or read his articles anymore, I knew he would never be done with politics. It gave him too many opportunities to go to conferences where many take a vacation from their jobs, their morals, and their spouses.

Where there is one, there is many.

BRANDON

the
Nondenominational
Believer

33

After the free market organization I had been working for closed up, I had a lot more free time on my hand. Maybe it was time to try online dating again. The first guy I met described himself as a "committed Christian." He was close to his family. He was tall and in his late thirties. We met at a nearby bagel shop. I was sitting at the table when he came in. He was wearing black pants and a black polo shirt. This combination was a pet peeve of mine. No two pieces of cotton black clothing ever go together. He was kind of sweaty, later explaining that we were close to his house so he had walked there.

I've always found most first dates aren't as awkward as their reputation. We know nothing about one another, so you can easily fill the time with questions. Of course, it is much more interesting when both people are asking the questions.

"What church do you go to?" I asked.

"I'm not really that religious," he said.

That was rather shocking given that he referenced "God" and "Jesus" in his profile more often than a rapper accepting an award. On Match.com and eHarmony, guys and girls lie about desiring long-term, committed relationships in order to attract members of the opposite sex. I guess on Christian dating sites, they lie about their commitment to God.

Truthfully, that didn't bother me as much as his total lack of interest in my life. I was growing tired of asking questions with no reciprocation. It was like talking to customer service at a department store.

"Are there restrooms near here?"

"Not really."

"Where are they?"

"Downstairs."

"What department?"

"Not sure."

After about an hour of my interview on banal life events, he asked if I could take him home because he had rheumatoid arthritis in his legs and couldn't make the walk himself. My first thought went to infamous Tallahassee resident and serial killer Ted Bundy, who walked with a cane in order to gain sympathy from women. I shook the thought out of my head and said it was fine.

Thankfully, he did only live a few minutes away. I parked in front of his apartment building.

"It was nice meeting you. Good luck on your trip to Alabama," I said.

"It's not for another month," he said.

Yeah, I knew that, I thought. It was a subtle way of saying I probably wouldn't see him again.

"There's one thing I want to tell you. I know it's not the most polite thing to say," he said.

"OK, what?" I asked.

"You have really nice breasts."

"Um, thank you."

"Do you think you could walk me to the door? I have to go up the stairs, and it's difficult for me."

"Oh, sure," I said. I walked him up the stairs and we hugged good-bye. We never saw one another again.

The Christian website seemed to have a sense of humor. One day it matched me with "A. Dike." Another time my "100 percent match" was someone who described the worst date he ever went on by simply saying, "She was overweight."

Another match was a small business owner and music producer. Given that he didn't live in New York, Los Angeles, or Nashville, I was leery of his music claims. After exchanging a few e-mails, we made plans to talk on the phone.

"What kind of music do you listen to?" I asked.

"I don't really listen to mainstream music," he said.

A few minutes in to the call, I already couldn't stand this guy. I continued the conversation just for the entertainment.

"What kind of work are you in?" he asked.

"Politics, I suppose. I'm a writer, and I do some communications and event consulting," I said.

"I understand politics on a much deeper level than anyone you know. I was basically groomed and on track to be a senator, but after seeing the inner workings of the political system, I left that world," he said matter-of-factly.

"Oh, how so?" I asked. I was now goading him for the sole purpose of telling friends about the time I talked to a crazy guy.

"Take the last presidential election. Do you actually think they let the average person pick the president? Look at who we had to choose from: a Muslim and a Mormon."

"So, who picks the candidates?" I asked.

"The people in charge. The Federal Reserve. That's why we need to print our own money."

"Are you a Ron Paul fan?"

"No. They know to have the crazy guy as their public enemy because no one will believe him. The only good candidate the Republicans have put forward in recent memory is John McCain."

"So, you're a Republican?"

"Yes, for all intents and purposes. Are you?"

"I am. I've been more involved on the grassroots conservative level than the campaign level, though. Right now the only group I'm involved with is for gay conservatives and their allies. There are some in the conservative movement who think gays don't belong, so I try to get people on their side," I told him.

"I agree with the people who don't want them in the movement. You can't be gay and conservative. Gays are violent and disgusting. But if they want to get married, let them get married," he said.

If I were talking with someone whose opinion mattered to me, this is where I would have started to get angry. Instead, I was just amused.

"What else do I not know?" I goaded.

"Do you know who will be the one to take our guns?"

"I don't know, Obama?"

"No, it will be the NRA, with the help of the federal agencies. The NRA has the largest list of gun owners," he said matter-of-factly.

As the call was winding down, he asked if we could meet for coffee the next day.

"Sure, we'll e-mail later and figure out a good place," I said. I fully intended to back out of this potential disaster.

The next morning I sent him an e-mail. "It was great to talk to you, but I think we're probably not a good match. Good luck with your search."

A few minutes later I got his response. "I agree. It is becoming clearer that I need a truly intelligent and educated woman. It is sad that you, and so many, are so entirely ignorant and unaware. Wishing me luck is about as hollow and fake a statement that could be made."

Of course I immediately shared his e-mail with my friends. A few months later he e-mailed. "I think we should talk again."

Needless to say, I didn't respond.

One night I was perusing my matches when one caught my eye. Supposedly we were a 99 percent match. He was a few years older, which I liked. He had sunglasses on in his main profile photo, so I clicked on "More Photos." He had six photos, and he was wearing sunglasses in all of them. Then I clicked on his profile introduction.

I am a federal employee, working in a position which provides new challenges and opportunities each day. I own a townhouse in the Fairlington area, where I have lived for the last two years. In addition to my many other characteristics, I also happen to be totally blind. Far from being the handicap that some people might perceive, this charac-teristic has increased my determination and drive to experience every-thing life has to offer and to not only live, but feel alive while doing so. Having achieved the goals of a federal career and home ownership, I am now looking for a special woman to be a part of my life. I realize that at my age most women will have children and I am certainly open to this possibility.

I am outgoing and adventurous, attempting to live life to the fullest. I enjoy taking on new challenges and overcoming fears. On one day, I may be parting the clouds skydiving from 13,000 feet, while on another I will sing a little Marvin Gaye at a karaoke establishment or participate in a church choir. I completed a mini triathlon a few years ago, and plan to complete one in the next few months. By contrast, I also enjoy more low-key, relaxing activities, such as movies, television, music and reading a few books a month.

I wondered if his profile ever caught women's attention or if most passed on him because he was blind. I knew the feeling of being rejected right out of the gate. Reading his profile, it didn't seem like his blindness was an obstacle. He had a job, owned a home, jumped out of an airplane, did a triathlon, read books, and enjoyed movies. As far as I could tell, his blindness only affected his ability to drive—and notice if I wore the same outfit twice.

I sent him a smile. It didn't seem to go through, so I sent it again. A few hours later, I received an e-mail from him.

"Thanks for your smile. A football fan? That's always a nice quality in a woman. Have you had much success with online dating?" he wrote.

I waited the customary few hours before responding. "I've met a couple people and talked to one on the phone, but no real success yet. You?"

"I've met a couple quality women, but nothing long-term yet. Would you like to talk on the phone? If so, send me your number and I'll give you a call so we can talk more and get to know one another," he wrote.

"Sure. I'll be working at a conference early next week, so evenings work," I wrote.

I had a temporary contract to do some on-site help and marketing for a political magazine's annual conference. I sat at the registration desk, handed people their nametags, and introduced some of the panels. It wasn't a totally menial job, but I did find it somewhat ironic that two years earlier I was named one of the magazine's "Rising Stars Under 35." I tried not to think about whether I was now a star that was rising or falling.

On the last day of the conference, I got a text message from Brandon. "I'll call you tonight at 7 p.m. Hope you're having a good day."

I like a guy with a plan. Whether it's dinner reservations, remembering birthdays, or setting a time to call, the ability to plan ahead separates the men from the boys.

Before I had a chance to respond, I realized that I was running late for introducing a panel on opposition research.

When the phone rang at 7:00 p.m. that evening, I had totally forgotten that Brandon would be calling me. "Hello?" I answered.

"Hi Lisa, it's Brandon."

"Oh, hi, nice to talk to you."

"I figured we could keep trading e-mails or just talk on the phone and see if we're a good match."

"That sounds like a fine idea," I said.

We exchanged pleasantries about our day and then talked more about online dating, religion, and the elephant in the room.

"I have to be honest, I was kind of surprised that you text and e-mail. Seeing how technology has become part of your life must be pretty amazing." I said. Whoops, I said *seeing*.

"It is. For the most part I can do anything anyone else can do with the exception of drive. And that's not far away because Google and others are working on self-driving cars."

"How do you get to work? The metro?"

"I take a bus to the King Street metro station and then metro into DC."

"Wow, I don't take the metro and I can see where everything is! Actually, because I can see everything is mostly the reason I don't take the metro," I joked.

"That's funny. You just get used it. Having an iPhone and Siri also help. After a while, you learn traffic patterns and rely on the sounds more than things like walk signals."

"You must really hate hybrids then. They don't make any noise."

"It's funny you say that because I almost got run over the other day when a hybrid ran a light."

"That's terrible. Have you thought about getting a Seeing Eye dog?" I asked.

"My mom wants me to get one, but I've always used a cane so that's what I'm used to."

"Let me know if I'm out of bounds on anything. I actually just find it fascinating that you have so much mobility," I said.

"It's no problem. I doubt you could ask anything that would offend me. I've heard it all."

"OK then," I said, "tell me the oddest question you've ever been asked."

"At a party once, a girl asked me if it was weird to have sex and not be able to see anything."

"That's a weird question, especially because you wouldn't have anything to compare it to."

"I asked her if she kisses with her eyes open or closed. Whenever people are being intimate, their eyes are closed. It's no different for me."

"No, that makes sense. It's a pretty dumb question," I said.

"People ask all kinds of things. Nothing really offends me," he said with a laugh.

"A part of me takes that as a challenge!" I said.

After an hour or so, we started talking about religion. He went to McLean Bible Church, a nondenominational megachurch. Their pastor was famous for running short commercials on the radio. His tagline was always, "Not a sermon, just a thought." I had attended one service there several years ago, but I was overwhelmed with the amount of people. It was one of those churches where they expect your social life to also revolve around the church. If you're single, there's a singles group. If you're married, there's a married group. If you're retired, there's a retired group. If you're a parent, there's a parent group. If you're married, retired, have kids, and have the Devil's red hair, there's probably a group for them, too.

"Do you participate in many of the social activities?" I asked.

"I've gone on a couple trips, and I have a group I do lunch with after Sunday school."

"I always say that my biggest hang-up with religion is religious people," I told him.

"I'm right there with you. I struggled with my Christian beliefs for a few years. Even now, there are times when I have to separate friends from things they say."

"In what way?" I asked.

"I've been at church events where people tell me that one day God will heal me and I'll be able to see, or that God will restore my sight in Heaven. I don't feel like I need to be healed, but I know they don't mean any harm by saying those things," he said.

"That's good that you don't take those things personally."

"You can't. Like I said, I'm not easily offended."

"That's good, because I can be offensive sometimes," I laughed.

"I love it!" he said. "I think we have a pretty good rapport and should meet up for a date in person."

"I agree. Do you have anything in mind?" I said.

"I was thinking Saturday. We could do dinner somewhere in Old Town and then karaoke."

"That sounds good, but you won't be getting me up on stage," I said.

After we hung up, I thought about what it would be like to date a blind guy. Imagine not having to obsess over every outfit. Slyly removing Spanx before getting intimate. Or not worrying about what you look like in the morning. So far, the only negative I could think of was that I would have to always be the one to drive.

34

During our phone call, I told Brandon about my interview column that asks right-leaning writers and entertainers fun, nonpolitical questions. I thought it would be interesting to send Brandon some of the questions and see how he fared. In the Internet age, you have to root out the guys who use shorthand that irked me like "u" and "ur" and "k." In an auto-correct and auto-fill world, there's no excuse for this foolishness. Since Brandon was blind, I decided I could give him a pass on "you're" versus "your."

One of my favorite answers from Brandon was to one of my frequent questions: "If you could be paid to do anything besides your current job, what would it be?"

As you can probably tell from our conversation last night, I have a passion for reading and especially making more titles available as e-books. This is perhaps due to the fact that as a kid I had very limited access to bestselling books that other friends were reading. I learned Braille at the same time you learned print, but often titles took years to be produced either in Braille or on cassette. Also, when a book was available on tape, it was usually abridged. With my speech synthesizer, I can read at a very fast rate. Depending on the size of the print, I can read the equivalent of a 300-page paperback in around four hours. I've noticed that occasionally publishers don't proofread their e-books when submitting them to Amazon, so in reading e-books I will often correct obvious scanning errors, grammatical errors, or typos. I'd love to read and correct manuscripts in order to ensure that customers get commercial-quality e-books for their money. This would also help to ensure that earlier titles in a series are available, as it's frustrating to see part of a series available as e-books but not earlier titles which are out of print.

It was a good, honest answer. This could work out, I thought. I was actually looking forward to our first date on Saturday and happy that he was taking the initiative to plan it. Brandon sent me an e-mail that afternoon.

A girl I've known for a year or two is moving out of the area to Florida with her boyfriend and wants to rent a limo for a small group and visit a few bars in Old Town to celebrate. She said I'm welcome to bring a date, and it'll probably happen Saturday, although I'm still waiting on her reply for the specific day and time. I realize you don't know me yet, so if this is too crazy to meet up for the first time, I understand and we can do something more casual like Joe Theismann's. Perhaps I don't need to say this, but I know that Christian Mingle doesn't do background checks, and I have nothing to hide if you feel the need to do one on me. I can appreciate that online dating can be a scary proposition for a woman, although you seem good at picking up on dishonesty and appear to have a low tolerance for bullshit. Anyway, I just thought I'd throw that out there, as I want you to be comfortable when we meet.

It was more information than I needed, but I appreciated more rather than less. I wrote back that it sounded fun and suggested that we meet somewhere thirty minutes or so ahead of time to chitchat before everyone else arrived. I thought it would be super awkward to have a group of people witness our first-date banter.

A few hours later, he suggested we meet up that night.

This is last minute, but since my weekend starts tonight, I thought I'd throw this out. The Fairlington Social Club, a meet-up group of which I'm a member, is meeting tonight in front of the Shirlington library for a music festival. Each week on Thursday they have a musical act, and this week it's jazz. Afterward we may walk to a nearby bar for an adult beverage. If this interests you, let me know, and I can add you as a guest. You'll want to bring a blanket or lawn chair.

So, now a blind date I had a few days to psych myself up for could happen tonight? Never has having a literal blind date come in so handy. I didn't have to worry as much about what to wear since it was a more casual setting. I e-mailed him back and we decided I would pick him up at his house and then we'd drive to the music festival.

Although going out with a blind man on a blind date did take the edge off, I would never leave the house without makeup and a flattering outfit. I settled on a white cotton blouse, red capris, and flowery espadrilles.

I was supposed to text him when I arrived at his house. It was a cute neighborhood. I had actually been there before. There was a motorcycle parked in the space he told me to park in. I wondered if its owner knew the space belonged to a blind guy and parked there often. The more I thought about it, the madder I got.

I texted Brandon that I was in the lot, but there was someone else parked in his spot. A few seconds later I saw him leave his house. He was wearing khaki shorts and a light-blue polo shirt. He flicked out his cane and walked down the sidewalk with purpose. I got out of my car and walked over to meet him at the end of the sidewalk.

"Hi there! Nice to meet you," I said.

"Great to meet you, too. I'm sorry someone was in the parking spot. I'll have to ask the neighbors about that."

I guided him to the passenger-side door.

"I guess I'll drive this time," I joked.

He laughed. The smart-ass in me wanted to test the theory that he was never offended.

The address for the music festival wasn't in my GPS, so he plugged it into his iPhone and had Siri take us there. He had programmed Siri to talk, like, five times faster than usual.

"Wow, it talks fast," I said.

"Yeah, I speed it up. I guess that's one of the benefits of being blind. I can understand things when sped up. When I listen to audiobooks, it's not recognizable to most people," he said.

"And you said you didn't have superpowers," I teased. During our phone call, he had said that a common misconception is that other senses are more powerful when you don't have the use of one.

He laughed and said, "No, I hear the same as everyone else. I don't have supersonic hearing or anything else."

A second after he said that, Siri spit out an indecipherable street name for me to turn on. Thankfully, he was holding the screen toward me and I could see that it was the next turn. He also continued to make small talk while I strained to listen to Siri. Who said he didn't have supersonic hearing?

We parked and got out of the car. I grabbed my bag with a blanket and a few bottles of water.

"So, which side do you prefer me to be on?" I asked.

"I'll be on your right," he said. "Do you have a bag you want me to carry? My mom used to load me up with grocery bags and call me her pack mule."

I laughed. "No it's fine. I just brought a bag with a blanket and some bottled waters."

"You were right, you are a planner."

"I can't help it," I said.

When we got to the festival area, I was happy to see there were plenty of tables and chairs. There were also some booths doing wine samples. The band was setting up, and I was reminded of when I used to go to Simon's shows. I almost always went alone and looked forward to the five minutes between sets when we were able to talk. It was nice to finally be at a show with someone.

"They have lots of tables and chairs set up, so we won't have to sit on the ground," I told him.

"Then the Fairlington group probably has an area," he said.

"Why don't we get a glass of wine and then find the group," I suggested.

We walked toward the booth as I tried to navigate a path that would allow us to still walk next to one another. It was a sunny day, so Brandon didn't stand out for wearing sunglasses. I wished he had his cane out so people would know to get out of the way.

At the wine booth, I read the descriptions of the various wines. I settled on a Riesling and he said he would have the same.

"Hey, Brandon, we're over here!" a man yelled.

"Oh, hey, Walter!" Brandon said as we walked closer.

Brandon said that he usually attended these weekly summer events. I couldn't imagine how he navigated around the area by himself. Going to these types of events were intimidating to an introvert like me. Even though I couldn't comprehend it, I had a lot of respect for Brandon's approach to life.

There was a group of four people at a long table. Brandon introduced me to the group as his date. After exchanging names that I soon forgot, Brandon and I talked about the area. The Fairlington area was situated between Arlington and Alexandria, Virginia. It was a fairly active and social group that enjoyed weekly activities in the area and at the clubhouse pool.

Once the music started, conversation was a little harder, so I moved closer to Brandon so I could hear him. I liked that every so often he would put his hand on my knee to make a point.

"What are you wearing?" he asked.

"Red capri jeans and a blouse," I said. I was immediately self-conscious about saying *red*. That couldn't have meant anything to him.

"I know in this kind of atmosphere casual is the way to go. I do like when women wear dresses," he said.

"I like dresses, too, but I figured since there was a chance we might be sitting on the ground it made more sense to wear pants," I said.

"That's smart. I'm sure you look very fashionable," he said.

As the music winded down, Walter suggested we go to a nearby Tex-Mex place for dinner. It was a nice night and not too hot, so our group of sixgrabbed a table outside.

"They have really good margaritas here," Brandon said.

"I think I'll just stick with Diet Coke this time," I said.

"Feel free to order anything you'd like. As I told you, I'm buying," he said.

I smiled. One thing I was starting to notice about Brandon was that he verbalized everything on his mind. I realized how many social cues relied on vision.

"I think I'll just have chips and salsa," I said.

As I approached the table after a quick trip to the restroom, Walter loudly said, "Welcome back, Lisa."

It couldn't have been more obvious that they had been talking about me while I was gone. After everyone else's margaritas were drained and the checks were paid, Brandon and I walked back to the car. Since it was now dark, I was unsure of the way back since we followed Walter on the way to the restaurant. It occurred to me that in addition to driving, if Brandon and I were in a relationship I would always have to be the one leading the way. I recalled the many times with Joe or Chris or Simon when I could just hand them the keys so they could drive and I wouldn't have to worry about it. I figured that could be a small price to pay for finding the right person.

"There's where the band was, so we must be heading in the right direction," I said.

"Yeah, I can't help much in that aspect," Brandon joked.

"So, what did you and Walter talk about when I left the table?" I asked.

"I asked him what he thought of you."

"And what did he say?"

"He said you were cute."

"Oh, he sounds smart," I said, laughing.

"So humble!" he said.

I drove Brandon back to his house. It was different to be the girl walking the guy to the door.

"Thanks for suggesting the music festival tonight. It was fun," I said.

"Oh, no problem. Like I said, they do these events every Thursday in the summer," he said.

"Well, let me get going since it's getting late. But give me a hug before I take off," I said.

"I'll be in touch about Saturday night. I think the limo thing is getting postponed, so we could just do dinner."

"That sounds good."

35

For our second official date, Brandon and I went to Hard Times Cafe in Old Town. After hearing the several hints he gave me about liking women in dresses, I wore a sleeveless black and white print dress.

"I'm wearing a dress this time," I told him.

"I'm sure you look beautiful," he said.

I asked him if he wanted me to read the menu to him. He declined and said he would get chili.

"Do you ever feel like you're missing out because you can't read the entire menu?" I asked.

"No, not really. This place is known for the chili, so I may as well get that."

"That's a good attitude. You mentioned in your profile that you read a lot of books. What do you like?" I said.

"I read all kinds of books. I like thrillers, like Brad Thor, and fantasy. I also like reading self-improvement and motivational-type books," he said.

"Funny you mention Brad Thor. I actually interviewed him for my column next week. I'm not really into fantasy, though. Unless you count *Harry Potter* or *The Hunger Games*."

"Those are good. You would like the fantasy series by Terry Brooks. There's a sarcastic talking dog in it."

I laughed. "Well, I like dogs and I like sarcasm."

"The other book you would like is *The Five Love Languages*. It's about the five different ways that people show love and how people need to know the language their significant other understands. Like for one person it might be hearing words of encouragement, and for another it might be receiving gifts."

"Who wouldn't want to receive gifts?"

"Well, yeah," he said.

After dinner we walked around the Alexandria waterfront. I remembered that the last time I was here it was with Adam. It was a cool night, so lots of people were walking around and taking advantage of the gorgeous weather. The park bench Adam and I sat on was empty. As Brandon and I walked around, I noticed people noticing him. We took a few photos of ourselves.

"Make sure you tell me where to look so I'm looking at the camera," he said.

It took a few tries, but we got a good photo before the sun went down.

"It's starting to get dark," I said. "Should we head over to the karaoke place?"

He pressed a button on his watch and held it up to his ear. "THE TIME IS 8:39 P.M.," it said.

"It doesn't really get started until 9:30, but we can go ahead and head over," he said.

"Sounds good," I said.

Coincidentally, Brandon's karaoke bar of choice was the place where I first met up with Adam when I came back from Florida. After living in the DC area for over fourteen years and having relationships with men I wanted to forget, there were some parts of town that felt off-limits. For years I didn't go to my favorite Chinese restaurant because Chris the Atheist would e-mail from time to time to ask for the name of it, confirming that he still went there. I avoided a Mexican restaurant near my office for months after I saw Joe the Catholic there with his wife and baby. Adam was Arlington. It was now a ghost town that I pretended didn't exist.

We settled into a table at the karaoke bar and ordered drinks.

"Do you know what you're going to sing?" I asked.

"Probably something by Journey. I did "In Da Club" by 50 Cent a few nights ago. You'll see when I go up that the crowd knows me pretty well."

It occurred to me that he must have memorized all these songs. Impressive. Also slightly dorky.

"Well, you're not going to get me up there," I said.

"I'll let you off the hook this time," he said.

"I'm going to go to the restroom. I'll be right back. Watch my purse!" I said.

"Smart-ass. I love it!" he said.

When it was Brandon's turn to sing, I led him up to the stage. His first song was "Shook Me All Night Long" by AC/DC. The crowd was definitely into it. He sounded good, but his voice was a little high. Odd, since he had a deeper speaking voice. As soon as he was done, I raced up to the stage so I could lead him back to the table.

"That was really good!" I said.

After karaoke we drove back to Brandon's house. I walked him inside. I was impressed with his place. The walls were painted. There was artwork, and it was fairly neat. I figured it was easier for him to be neat so he knew where everything was when he needed it.

"Well, thank you for dinner and drinks," I said.

"You're welcome. I'm glad you got to see me do karaoke," he said.

"It was fun!" I said.

We hugged and then, to fill the awkward space, I gave him a peck on the lips.

"I wasn't expecting that!" he said.

I laughed. "OK, well, we'll talk soon."

The next morning, I was surprised to see that Brandon had gifted me the books he talked about on our date. It was very thoughtful, and I was impressed.

"Thank you so much for the books!" I texted him.

"You're welcome. I'd be interested in knowing what you think of them," he responded.

"I definitely will let you know."

"I was thinking of hitting the pool today. I know your tan is important to you. Do you want to go?"

"That sounds good. I posted the photo from last night on Facebook so your mom could see it," I said.

"When I talked to her this morning she said you were cute. She's been reading your articles and your Twitter."

"Uh-oh, I'll have to be good from now on," I joked.

"I didn't know you were so racy," he said.

"I'm just kidding. I'm always good."

"And always modest, too."

"It's not bragging if it's true," I teased.

"I do know women can be blunt, if not cruel, at times. I just saw a Facebook posting from a girl I know who saw your picture of us at the waterfront. She thought you were chunky. I know weight is a sensitive issue for women, and this is not a deal-breaker, but I just thought the comment was rather insensitive," he wrote.

Really? How many times did he have to solicit other people's opinions about my looks? And why did he feel like he had to tell me the hurtful things people said?

"In the future, you don't need to tell me the negative things your friends think about me," I wrote.

"You have accomplished a lot, professionally and personally, and I would be remiss if I didn't take all that into account. I will not give up on a woman for superficial reasons. I'm not in the shape I want to be in, but I will get there," he responded.

"Why do you think a friend of yours would write that?" I asked.

"It was a private message on Facebook. I don't know why she said that. I think she's biased toward Asian women and thinks I would look better with a blonde. She knew that I had gone out with a Filipina and she herself is Filipina. I think she is biased toward her own countrywomen."

"I just don't understand why someone else would care about someone else's looks. What was your response?" I asked.

"I told her that I will not make a shallow decision based solely on looks and will evaluate the whole person. Unfortunately, people can be very shallow."

The more he tried to explain, the angrier I got. "For God's sake, it's not like I'm an ogre or something. Trust me, I've had plenty of guys who were shallow and attracted to me. I don't need the fact that I've lost a lot of weight as a disclaimer. I'm attractive now. Do I want to lose more weight? Of course," I said.

I continued, "Guys never seem to realize that the phrase 'looks don't matter to me' is kind of an insult."

"You don't have to defend yourself to me. I like you the way you are," he said. "I'm sorry I mentioned that comment. I should've taken your feelings into account. I won't mention anything negative my friend says about you again. Are we cool?"

"Yes. I'm going to bed."

I plugged my phone into the charger and went upstairs to bed. I remembered something that I think Whittaker Chambers said. People don't get angry when you tell lies about them; they get angry when you tell the truth about them.

The negative feelings about my weight and looks in general were so ingrained in my mind that I was now dreading being in a bathing suit with a blind guy the next day.

36

On Sunday I drove to Brandon's house so we could spend a few hours at the pool. I picked up lunch on the way.

As we walked behind his house to the neighborhood pool, he squeezed the top of my right arm. "It feels like you're losing weight!" he remarked.

"OK," I said.

I was used to people saying that I looked like I had lost weight, but to hear someone say it *felt* like I was losing weight was outside my comfort zone.

"I think I'll do my laps first so I can get those out of the way since I still need to go to church today," he said.

"Sounds like a plan," I said.

"My dad says I'm crazy for getting involved with a woman who doesn't go to church every week," he said.

"OK, well I think he's crazy for marrying someone he's only known for six weeks."

He had told me that his father had also met someone on a dating site and after a few weeks of dating, he told Brandon and his brother that he was getting married. They hadn't met the mystery woman yet.

"I'm not saying that's how I feel; it's just something he said. He's very religious," he said.

"That's fine. I'm religious, but not the kind of religious that makes me judge people based on my own religious habits," I said.

This was starting to be a pattern with Brandon. He had a tendency to say things without considering other people's feelings. And he talked a lot. I gave him a pass on that because he experienced the world verbally. Yes, it was annoying that he narrated things like petting a dog, but on the plus side, I could show up for a day at the pool without a smidgen of makeup.

I felt bad that I looked forward to the quiet time while I sunbathed and listened to music without Brandon asking if the song I was listening to was this or that. (Hello, super hearing powers!)

When Brandon got out of the pool after forty impressive laps, I met him at the edge and walked him back to the chairs.

After a few hours at the pool, we walked back to his place. I was feeling a little nauseous from being out in the sun and not drinking enough water. "Do you mind if I lay down for a bit?" I asked.

"No, not at all," he said.

We went upstairs and I climbed on top of the bed. He laid down flat on his back.

"Let me get in your nook," I said.

"My nook?"

"Yes, lift your arm and I'll get right here," I said, touching his side.

I got in the nook and stayed there for almost an hour. We kissed. He giggled when I used my tongue. "You like to use your tongue," he said.

"Yeah, most people do. Do you not like it?"

"It's not that. I'm just surprised," he said.

"Then stop giggling!" I said, laughing. I was trying to keep my tone playful, but he was really annoying. It was like kissing a twelve-year-old boy. Actually, a twelve-year-old boy would have had a lot more interest in my breasts than Brandon did. Was it because he couldn't see them and appreciate them, or was he just not interested?

Brandon loved talking about relationships, including our current status of not being exclusive.

"You know, I know we're not exclusive. You don't need to keep reminding me," I said.

"I just want to be honest. I think that being exclusive is on the way to marriage, and I'm not there yet," he said.

"I'm not either," I said. "I guess I just don't think exclusivity necessarily means you're on the marriage track. I think it just means you're not sleeping with other people. At this point, we're not sleeping with one another, so I don't consider us exclusive either. All I'm saying is that I don't need to be reminded that you don't have those feelings for me yet. It's insulting."

"OK, I understand where you're coming from," he said.

37

Brandon and I had been dating for almost two months. He met Thomas, my former assistant, when I took them both to Kings Dominion amusement park. I was nervous about Thomas meeting Brandon. Thomas and I were so close, like a big sister and a little brother, that others sometimes bristled at the way we talked to one another.

I invited Thomas because he liked roller coasters and was willing to go on all the rides that Brandon wanted to go on. Thomas also benefitted from Brandon being able to cut the lines and go to the handicapped entrance.

By the end of the day, I was exhausted from being in the hundred-degree heat and walking in circles in order to hit every coaster. After I dropped Brandon off at his house, I drove Thomas back to my house so he could get his car.

I pulled into the garage and said, "Well, Thomas, this was quite a day."

"It was fun. We probably had more fun than you did, though," he said.

"I had fun because I wasn't made to do anything I didn't want to do, despite you and Brandon trying."

"Can we hang out a bit and talk?"

"Sure, let's go inside. I'm dying for a Diet Coke," I said.

Thomas sat on my living room rug while I settled into my big red chair.

"So, what did you think of Brandon?"

"He seems nice."

"What else?"

"Well, I just don't think he can keep up with you. You know, the way we talk. I don't think he gets how sarcastic we are."

"Yeah, I know what you mean. But maybe that's a side of me that only you and close friends see. I don't have to be that way with the guy I'm dating. I mean, I'm not going to talk to him like I talk to you. When he's looking for his cane, I'm not going to be like 'Hurry up, dummy' like I would with you."

Thomas laughed. "There's no way you could keep your sarcastic side hidden for that long."

"Maybe so," I said.

"Oh, I also didn't like how he kept dwelling on the fact that you didn't want to ride anything. He said he was really disappointed you didn't go on more than one coaster."

"That's dumb. I was pretty up front about it. That's the whole reason I invited you. Since y'all can go together, there's no point in me being miserable and doing something I don't want to do."

"I know. He just seemed to dwell on it," Thomas said.

"Yeah, that happens sometimes. He repeats himself a lot. But I don't know if it matters or it's just that I notice it."

"I don't know what that means," he said.

"I mean, should I care about whether a guy is repetitive? It's not like I have other potential dates lined up around the block."

Thomas sighed loudly. "Lisa, you should be with someone you like and who is compatible with you. You know him better than I do. I was just saying what I thought after spending only one day with him."

Then he added, "But, the problem with the everyday annoyances is that they're every day."

After Thomas left, I thought about what he said. Was I really willing to be in a relationship with a guy who checked all the boxes of a "good man"—has a job, owns a house, goes to church—even though he didn't get me?

As always, it's the intangible things that make or break a relationship. Most of the time, I didn't feel like Brandon and I had chemistry. I also wanted to feel attractive. Or be told I was attractive, I suppose. When I told my sister that the guy I was seeing was blind, she said, "It's a shame that he'll never see how beautiful your eyes are."

I wanted to meet someone from the Christian dating site because I was still looking for religious guidance. I found myself disappointed that Brandon only seemed interested in the routine of church rather than the Word. He didn't invite me to church or offer any advice on Christian books to read.

With the exception of Thomas, I think everyone liked us together because it meant I had finally found someone. Christine liked Brandon. I couldn't help but notice that even though they didn't know one another, she was very eager and happy about me being with him.

Brandon's mother was elated but skeptical. After meeting her and her husband, Brandon told me his mother asked if he was sure he had enough to offer me. Mothers ALWAYS liked me.

Because of various circumstances, it had been two weeks since we had seen one another. We texted every few days, but it was clear that something was off. Earlier in the week we had talked about me taking him to Costco for his monthly staples.

"Are you still up for Costco?" he wrote.

"Sure," I responded. A lot of our outings were starting to revolve around errands. Trips to the drugstore. Me picking up lunch before going to the pool. Me picking up various things when I happened to be out doing my own errands—an item from the grocery store, a watch battery.

"Great! Why don't we go to lunch first?"

"Sounds good. I'll pick you up around noon."

Today was going to be the day. I would bring up the issue of whether we should continue to date. I was open to the possibility, but I wanted to be with someone who wanted to share his life and his faith, not just his errand list.

When I arrived at Brandon's house, he said he had several of my dishes cleaned. I gave him the leftover brownies I made for Christine's barbeque and a container of sauce and meatballs I made him. I didn't have anything else at his house, so it was likely I wouldn't need to come back if the conversation went a certain way.

I drove us to a restaurant near the Costco in my neighborhood. After ordering, I decided it was time to have the conversation we had been avoiding.

"Over the last two weeks, do you feel like you haven't seen your girlfriend or that you haven't seen your friend?" I asked.

"Yeah, I've been meaning to talk to you about that. It does feel more like a friendship," he said.

"Look, I think you're a good guy and I'm a good girl, but that doesn't mean we have to be together. It's OK if things just don't work out," I said.

"There's something missing. I guess I thought there would be more romantic feelings."

As usual, Brandon was belaboring the point. I didn't need a dissertation on his feelings and how I wasn't enough. It was mutual. I didn't see any point in telling him that I wanted someone who was more considerate, wasn't self-righteous about what made a good Christian girl, and a partner in love and life. But I let him say his piece.

He continued, "It's just I keep thinking about what you said about how your ex-boyfriends say you're the one who got away, and I wonder if I'm making a mistake."

That's where I had to interrupt him. "This isn't one-sided," I said. "Things are missing for me, too. It's OK that it isn't working out. We both feel like this isn't what we're looking for in a relationship and that's OK."

He didn't seem to hear me when I said I wasn't willing to continue in this relationship. Still, we had a respectful conversation. I suppose it was a lot easier since we never had to make eye contact.

"Well, I guess I'll still take you to Costco," I jokingly said.

He laughed. I don't think it ever occurred to him that I wouldn't.

As we pushed the cart around Costco, Brandon worked through the set list of things he always got: bananas, muffins, bread, Dr. Pepper, and turkey. He was oblivious to the other options in the huge warehouse. He had his list of things to get, nothing more and nothing less. I suppose in his head he had a list of the attributes of a perfect mate and how he would feel about her. I didn't fulfill that list, and for the first time in my life, that was OK with me. I also knew what I wanted in a man, and I was willing to wait for him rather than become whoever someone else wanted me to be.

Mr. Righteous

38

After things fizzled out with Brandon, I turned my focus to job hunting and writing. I was doing more for various conservative websites, as well as handling my own writing projects. I've been fortunate to have several encouraging mentors over the years. I never forgot how important it was to be noticed and encouraged by people I admired. When people e-mailed me looking for the same encouragement, I was usually happy to have a productive back-and-forth and share with them my thoughts about writing and the conservative movement.

One evening, a follower on Twitter asked if I would follow him so he could send me a direct message. His name was Hunter. His profile photo was of him shooting a gun, so he seemed trustworthy. I followed him and sent him a direct message. "Here I am," I wrote.

He wrote back, "Thanks for following me! I was wondering if I could send you an e-mail with a few questions."

I told him that was fine and gave him my e-mail address. I generally protected my e-mail address because I didn't want to end up on random lists or be hounded by random people. For some reason, I didn't hesitate when he asked.

A few days later, he sent me an e-mail.

Lisa,

Thank you so much for taking the time to answer a few questions. My main query would definitely be, who should I be looking to hook up with / learn from if my goal is to eventually do what Breitbart did?

I've heard that starting a blog and writing every day is the first step, but how do I get noticed?

It seems to me that, at least on Twitter, many of the most influential people in this movement run with each other in real life. How does one go about getting the attention of the gang (for the purpose of learning from them because "iron sharpens iron") and what's the etiquette in dealing with those I want to befriend / learn from?

I feel like I have a voice and I believe that it is a gift. I don't want to waste it. Now just what the heck do I do with it?

Hunter

I use to receive at least one e-mail like this a month, but they had slowed to a trickle as my involvement in the conservative movement waned. I was less political on Twitter and in my writing, choosing instead to write about culture and on reaching out to those outside the activist class. However, it was still nice to know that others looked to me for advice on being a successful writer, especially when I was feeling less than successful as I looked for a full-time job.

A few days later I wrote Hunter back.

Hi there,

Definitely the first step is to write something every day. I think in this day and age, blog posts don't have to be every day as long as you're interacting on social media. The second thing is to be proactive in sharing other people's articles. It helps foster good relationships with other writers. I've always tried to be available for favors and such because you never know when someone can be helpful to you.

As far as getting in good with influencers, I think the same rings true. Tweet their articles, engage them. Your first approach to someone shouldn't be "You might like this [link to something you wrote]." They probably get dozens of those a day.

When you write, link back to others, maybe let them know you quoted them in an article. We're all egotists at the end of the day :)

I hope this helps. Let me know if I can help with anything else!

Lisa

He soon e-mailed that he appreciated me. It was nice to hear, especially at a time when I thought I had nothing left to offer the conservative movement.

39

By September, Hunter and I regularly conversed on Twitter. He was funny and was good about listening to radio interviews I did and linking to my latest columns. After a night of going back and forth about being more active in the conservative writing community, he asked if he could have my number so we could talk on the phone instead.

An hour or so later I got a call. The caller ID had a woman's name, so I hesitantly answered the phone.

"Hello?"

"Hi, this the Tea Party organization. We're calling to see if you're interested in donating?"

"Umm . . ."

"I'm just kidding. It's me, Hunter."

"Oh, hi, you got me. I'm so sick of getting those calls. Also, a different name comes up on my caller ID."

He had a nice, southern accent. It wasn't a good ol' boy accent, but a guy who holds the door open for the elderly accent. As we talked, it became clear that he saw a lot of conservative writers and activists, especially those like Andrew Breitbart, as heroes. Having spent over fourteen years working in conservative circles, I had become cynical and jaded about the movement. It was interesting to view it through his eyes. The people I had seen falling-down drunk or begging for a speaking slot on a panel were stars in his eyes. I didn't want to rain on his parade, but I also felt the need to be honest with him.

As we talked, he mentioned there was a girl he had gotten to know from Twitter and that he would be meeting her in person soon.

"She knows you. She really respects you," he said.

"Oh, who is it? Have I met her?" I asked.

"Her name is Kaitlyn. She lives in Texas."

"Oh, yeah, I met her at a blogger party a few years ago. She seems cool."

"She is. I really like her a lot."

"When are you going to meet up with her to see if things can progress?

"This weekend. We'll both be in the same city. I know there's something there, though. She looks at me like she wants to have my kids."

"That's pretty serious," I said.

"I haven't always been the most godly man, but over the last year or so I've tried to rededicate myself to God. I want to be righteous for the right woman," he said.

"That's awesome," I said.

"For real, I don't even look at photos of her on Facebook where cleavage or her body is showing because I don't want to have lustful thoughts about her."

Hunter was a good man. I was encouraged by his words of faith and commitment to being the kind of man he thought the girl he liked deserved.

When it came time for Hunter to meet up with his dream girl, he was excited and I was excited for him. We had talked often enough that I cared about him and wanted him to be happy.

By the weekend, Hunter was on the road and his meeting with Kaitlyn was imminent.

"Plans with Kaitlyn this weekend? I have to live through your exploits since I have none of my own," I said.

"She's working at events all day tomorrow, but hopefully I'll see her on Sunday. I sent her a video I did with my buddy's daughter. I'll send it to you."

I watched the video and it was pretty adorable. He was trying to get the daughter to do a shout-out to Kaitlyn. Her words were more like funny sounds. A man said something off-camera and Hunter doubled over in laughter. I remembered when Chris the Atheist told me that he hated that I covered my mouth when I laughed. I did it because I was self-conscious about my chubby cheeks. I was drawn to Hunter's ability to just laugh freely and completely. I realized I wanted to make him laugh like that one day.

"That's so cute. A man with a kid! You know how to hit a girl's soft spot."

"I mean I might be trying. A little," he said.

"She is pretty adorable."

"I don't care how sleepy you are, when a five-year-old pokes you in the back and says 'Hunter, WAKE UP!' you have to get out of bed and hang out with her," he said.

The next day I texted Hunter to find out how his first meeting with Kaitlyn went. "Well . . . how did it go?" I asked.

"It was fun. I met her for coffee after the baseball game and then we went to dinner with my friends. It was a good day."

Unfortunately, his optimism didn't last. The next morning he called while I was at the doctor's office.

"Can't talk. At the doctor's office," I texted.

"No problem. I hope all is well. I just wanted to chat. Leaving Dallas in a bit and my heart is heavy. It happens," he said.

"Why?"

"Lots of reasons. I love it here. My friends that I made in my twenties, the real ones, are all here. Plus, I'm meeting Kaitlyn for coffee on the way back. I'm not sure that's gonna turn out like I'd hoped. Not right now anyway."

"I should be home in thirty minutes or so if you want to talk," I told him.

"I would really, really like that," he wrote.

When Hunter answered the phone, I said, "OK, lay it on me."

"She wouldn't meet with me. I'm leaving Dallas now. 'Take me back to Tulsa, boys, I'm too young to marry.' You know that song?" he said.

"It sounds like a country song, so probably not. So, what do you mean? No coffee?"

"She said she was too busy. I'm just really disappointed that I came all this way and she knew 85 percent of the reason was to see her and she couldn't make time."

"Did you have concrete plans?" I asked.

"Yeah, she was supposed to go to the baseball game with me, but she backed out of that. She at least came to dinner and that was good."

"Was the dinner good? Was it awkward at all because you met her for the first time with other people there?" I asked.

"No, it wasn't awkward at all. Except when she made a big deal about me paying. My buddy and his wife said we acted like we had known one another for years."

"That's good. Maybe she really was just busy," I said.

"I'm sure she is, but when she said she couldn't meet me for coffee, I said I'd bring coffee to her and she vetoed that. I know she's had some issues with men in her past, but I've been nothing but nice. I'm not pushing her into anything. I just want to get to know her outside of the phone and Skype."

"I don't think you've done anything wrong. Some people just have their own baggage or reason for doing things."

"Yeah, I know. I just wanted to show her that I care and that I like her. Her birthday is next week, so I'm just going to send her a card and a gift card to this running place she mentioned."

"That's very thoughtful. Are you sending flowers, too? Girls love that stuff. Especially if it's to their work and they can show them off," I said.

"I thought of that, but her birthday is on a Saturday. I think since we left things kind of up in the air, I should just do the gift card."

Apparently, Kaitlyn and I had a different opinion on birthday gifts.

Hunter called me a few days later and he was crestfallen. "So, she got the gift card early. She basically just sent me a text that attacked me for doing it. She said she hates gifts and all that sort of thing. She said she didn't mean to be ungrateful, but geez," he said.

"That is weird. Her ex or her family really did a number on her," I said.

"Yeah, I've got a knot the size of a football in my stomach right now. I can't tell if my feelings are hurt or if I'm angry."

"Just remember it's not about you. People have their issues. If you were to treat her like crap, that might be more familiar and comfortable to her, but that doesn't make that behavior right. Likewise, being nice and giving a gift doesn't make your behavior inappropriate or wrong just because she's making you feel that way," I told him.

"Honestly, this kind of lets the air out of my balloon. It makes me feel like I shouldn't even try with her. Or with writing or anything."

"This has nothing to do with writing. If I tell you to scram, then, yeah, you probably should stop trying," I joked.

"I'm so something right now. I think it's mad."

"I think you're probably more disappointed than mad. You put thought into a gift for someone you care about and the reaction didn't match what you put into it."

"That's an understatement," he said, sighing.

My heart was breaking for him. He might not have been sure if he was mad, but I knew I was. Over the last few weeks, I had gotten to know Hunter pretty well. He was such a good, honest guy. I was angry that a girl he really had feelings for couldn't see what she was missing out on.

"Listen, I know it sucks, but I think you really need to step back and let things start or end naturally and not be proactive. For whatever reason, that bothers her. I promise you that this isn't your last chance at finding someone," I said.

"I know, I know. I just don't understand what the heck happened," he said.

"She's pushing you away, plain and simple. Maybe she sensed there were expectations there. Like she had to be the perfect date in person that she is on the phone or via text. When someone is really into you, it's a lot to live up to."

"But I didn't have any expectations. I just wanted to do a nice thing."

"Well, at least we have a definitive answer on whether or not to send flowers," I joked.

He laughed.

40

Hunter was still struggling with how things ended with Kaitlyn. After a particularly harsh phone call with her, I tried to comfort him. I had been in the same situation before, and I knew that dwelling on it never helps.

"I don't know if this will make you feel better, but tonight is the worst you'll feel. Things will get better," I said.

"You're my friend, Lisa. I'm thankful for you. Now if you could get the *Red Eye* guys to follow me on Twitter," he said.

"Twitter doesn't matter. If they met you, they'd like you in real life."

"Now you're just trying to make me feel better. Don't stop. It's working."

Despite only being in regular communication for a few weeks, Hunter and I leaned on one another. Some days it wasn't equal, and that was OK. He still thought of me as some conservative mover and shaker and joked about me introducing him to other writers or women on TV. But when I was feeling down, I wasn't a writer that could get him published or linked by Twitchy. I was just a friend.

The next day he said, "Have you gotten the feeling that we met at exactly the right time? Like just when each of us needed someone to lean on, who would lean back, thus preventing a collapse."

"I think that's a good way to look at it," I said.

"I'm not ashamed to admit that I needed someone who would get me. And then along came Lisa," he said. "Also, you were right. Last night was as bad as I'm going to feel."

"Get used to saying that first part," I said.

"That you're right?"

"Yep!"

"Even though I feel better, I'm going to watch *The Notebook* tonight and eat a whole thing of ice cream by myself," he said.

"It's nothing to be ashamed of," I said. "Just never, ever tell any girl who you want to be sexually attracted to you."

"Ever? Got it."

"I'm just kidding. Some girls are into soft guys."

"I'm not really soft. I do have a big heart, though."

"All girls like that . . . Oh, you said heart," I joked.

He laughed. "You're all right, Lisa."

Later that night I met up with some friends at a local bar. After having two drinks too many, I walked back to my friend Dan's office so I could sober up. As we sat in his office, it occurred to me that he knew Ryan the Preacher and Adam the Jew. I opened up about everything. I was soon crying about how I had let these guys sucker me into thinking they cared about me.

The next morning, as I sat at my computer checking e-mail, I thought about Hunter and my conversation with Dan the previous night. And an amazing thing happened. I realized that I was just as much to blame for my behavior with Adam and Chris as they were. I acted like I was a victim of these religious and relationship hypocrites, but I was no better. I hadn't been behaving like a girl who deserved the kind of guy I wanted. I thought of Hunter. There were times when he made mistakes in his personal life, like everyone, but he was a man of God. He was a Mr. Righteous.

I had spent so much time thinking about the kind of man I wanted that I didn't look inward and try to be the woman a Mr. Righteous deserved. C. S. Lewis wrote that free will was proof that there was a God. He gives us what we think we deserve. Even though I said I was looking for a Mr. Righteous, I was content with scraps from Ryan and Adam because I felt like that was all I deserved.

I felt God—the real Him in my life—at that moment. He gave me the strength to know that it was OK to walk away from my past. I was no longer afraid of losing someone who didn't care about me. I had Him.

I couldn't wait to tell Hunter.

41

I told Hunter about my epiphany of being the Miss Righteous a man like him deserved. Even when I confessed my part in seducing Ryan or Adam, he didn't put me down. He told me that he had the same struggles with women. He confessed that he had a moment of weakness the night before and had been with a girl he had no interest in pursuing. He said he wanted to recommit himself to God. To be the Mr. Righteous I thought he was.

It was hard to believe we had only been talking for a month. A lot of our communication had been me giving him the scoop on the drama and personalities in the conservative movement and supporting his writing. He often told me how much he appreciated me helping him. It's always been hard for me to be vulnerable and rely on other people. That night I wanted him to know that I was appreciative of him. Since he was out of town, I sent him an e-mail.

Dearest Hunter,

I just wanted to take a few minutes and tell you how glad I am to know you. I think you're right about us connecting at exactly the right time.

I was so happy when you told me about your last 24 hours. Sometimes I feel like when I have those same thoughts (like wanting to strengthen my relationship with God), I feel like a fake or even unworthy. I know it's a daily affirmation or decision we have to work toward. It makes it A LOT easier knowing I have a friend with the same struggles and desires.

I just wanted to let you know that I appreciate and value your friend-ship. You're living the life I value the most—a real man of God. Every-thing else that happens outside of that in the movement or with your writing will be great, but you're already a bigger and better person than anything else you could dream of in that area.

Best, Lisa

A few hours later, Hunter e-mailed me back.

You know, I was thinking this earlier, so I'll go ahead and say it. I'm glad we're friends. I have no idea what you see in me or why you like me. I'm not being down on myself, it's just that so many people must come to you. Why you picked me is a mystery. I'm incredibly blessed to have you in my life, Lisa.

I'm going to tell you how much you mean to me. You wake me up almost every morning. Everyone who knows me knows not to text or call me in the morning. I even told Kaitlyn not to text me in the morning. But you wake me up and I don't mind.

That afternoon I called Hunter.

"I'm never texting you in the morning again," I said.

"No! I don't want you to change! I was just using that as a metric to measure how much you mean to me," he said.

"You might be my best friend, Hunter."

"Seriously?" he said.

"Yes. Is that weird?" I asked.

"No, I just think about a lot of other people who came before me and had the chance to be close to you and have missed out. And it's their loss."

"As long as you think so."

"I do and when I see you I'm going to give you a big ol' hug"

"No!" I said. "I'm not a hugger!"

"You're getting it, De Pasquale. A bear hug and you're going to have to deal with it."

"We'll see. You know, there's a Bible verse I read this morning that made me think of you. I e-mailed it to you so I wouldn't wake you up."

"I read it. That is a good one," he said. "Who took notice of who?"

"Both of us, I think," I said. "You know, I feel so behind in my faith because I don't know many Bible verses or stories."

"You shouldn't feel that way."

"What are your favorites?" I asked.

"The Psalms are good. David wrote a bunch of them. He's proof that anyone can be a vehicle for God's word."

"Why is that? I thought David was good?" I said.

"Well, King David was called a man after God's own heart. He was the greatest king of Israel and was one of the forefathers of Christ. But he also did a terrible thing and he was a fallen man," Hunter told me.

I was hesitant to ask too many questions. I was so used to being judged for my lack of Biblical knowledge. "What terrible things?" I asked.

"Do you know who Bathsheba was?"

"Um, the name is familiar," I said.

"It's OK. So, Bathsheba was a beautiful woman that King David seduced. The only problem with this was the fact that she was another man's wife. Oh, and David had that other man killed to conceal his actions, but I'll get to that."

"Tell me everything," I said. "Start with 'In the beginning.'"

Hunter laughed. "David was one of Israel's greatest military leaders, but at one point, instead of doing what he was supposed to be doing and going to war with his own army, David stayed home. This would've been a first step of disobedience and of laziness. This would've definitely been a slap in the face to the armies of Israel. He's like, 'Hey, you guys go fight and I'm gonna sit this one out at home.'"

He continued, "So one day while David is roaming around the palace there in Jerusalem, he decides to take a trip to the roof and while there, he sees from his vantage point a woman bathing on her own roof.

"Now, she was beautiful and David was quite taken with her, so David sent for her. He found out who she was and brought her to his palace. She was already married, but that did not matter to David. He lusted after her and he wanted her. As it turns out, Bathsheba was the wife of Uriah the Hittite. Uriah was one of the champions of David's army. That did not stop David, though. He slept with Bathsheba anyway. Which makes you think, you know, what kind of woman was Bathsheba?

"But I digress, we're focusing on David at this point. So, at any rate, Bathsheba conceived a child and David knew this would be big trouble. Instead of doing the right thing, he sent for Uriah to come home from battle and spend some time with his wife. David encouraged Uriah to go to his wife and he figured, things being as they were, that Uriah and Bathsheba would sleep together and Uriah would eventually end up thinking that David's child was actually his own. However, Uriah was a man of integrity and of honor and of valor. He refused to do what David expected. Uriah refused to go to his wife while his men were still in the field. He felt it was dishonoring his vows to the army, and he refused to break those vows," Hunter said.

"I like listening to you tell stories," I said.

"Thank you. I like telling you. So, instead of going to Bathsheba, Uriah slept on his own front doorstep. When his first plan failed, David decided to kill Uriah. David wrote a letter giving orders to have Uriah placed at the forefront of the fighting and when the fighting grew to its fiercest, David ordered that the men should pull back from Uriah so that he would be struck down. Here, David commits what was ultimately one of the most evil acts ever.

"In his next move, he writes this letter, seals it with his own emblem, and then sends this letter back to the front lines with Uriah. Uriah trusted David and was loyal to David and in return, David sent Uriah back to the front lines carrying his own order of execution."

"That is pretty cold," I said.

"As you might expect, Uriah gets back and hands the letter to his superiors, who do exactly as David has commanded—they put him at the front lines and then when the fighting is at its fiercest, they pull back from Uriah and Uriah is killed," he continued.

"After this, David brings Bathsheba into the palace as one of his own wives. Now, the prophet Nathan comes to King David and in a very beguiling plot twist, he begins to tell the king a story. Nathan tells the story of a rich man who stole from a poor man. He says, 'King, in your land there is a rich man who has everything. Many horses, many cattle, many oxen, many donkeys, a nice house, a lot of land, and a big family. Next door to this rich man, lives a very poor man whose family has only a single lamb.' This lamb provides certain necessities for the family, but it is also like a pet to the man and his children. Now, the rich man covets what the poor man has, even though the rich man has plenty. He wants what the poor man has, so he steals the lamb from the poor man, kills it, and has it for dinner. He wants it, so he just takes it and he kills it."

"So, he's, like, trolling King David?" I asked.

"Exactly! Upon hearing this, David flew into a rage. He was so angry that he demanded to know who the rich man was. David demanded that he be found and brought to justice for what he had done. David felt the rich man should be put to death. So the prophet Nathan looks David squarely in the eyes and says, 'It's you, motherf*****. You did this.'

"Nathan explains that what David has done in taking the wife of Uriah and then having Uriah killed is the very same as what the rich man had done to the poor man. David is immediately humbled. He's grieved and brokenhearted. There is no bringing Uriah back. There is no way to not have slept with Bathsheba. There is no way to undo what has already been done, but David does repent. He tears his clothes off and sits in ashes and seeks the face of God."

"Wow," I said.

"So, David repents and he is forgiven, but there are consequences. David's house falls into a disarray of sorts, ultimately leading to the downfall of many of his own children. Even worse, the child that he conceived with Bathsheba dies. There are consequences for the sins that he committed. However, the Lord does not forsake David. He continues to walk with David as David walks with Him, and He honors David as David honors Him. God does not throw David to the wolves or turn His back on David, even though David turned his back on God."

Just like me, I thought. I turned my back on God for years. Then, even as a self-proclaimed Christian, I did things I shouldn't have done.

Hunter continued, "The lesson here is that if somebody like David can be called a man after God's own heart after doing such a terrible thing—something that we would condemn him for—how deep and how wide is the love and forgiveness of God that was offered to us through Christ? That's the point of the story."

"I think you should definitely tell me a Bible story every night. 'MFers' and all," I said.

"Yeah, I realized that I dropped an 'MFer' into a Bible story and while I'm not saying this flippantly, God would even forgive me for that, so you see the point very clearly illustrated before you in the form of my getting worked up telling you a story and using a swear word that obviously was not written into the pages of the Bible. There is forgiveness for even those such things."

He added, "Now I don't use this story to excuse myself or give myself permission to do whatever I choose. I only use the story to illustrate the point that when we are truly sorry and truly repentant, God never fails us. He always takes us back, He always forgives us, and He always sees us as His children who He loves."

After we hung up, I got ready for bed. I thought about Hunter's Bible story. He wasn't pretentious or judgemental when I asked questions or joked that David was trolling. I thought about the other men in my life who I had reached out to for religious guidance. I always felt less than worthy, like having questions about Bible verses, seeking religious guidance for the wrong reasons, or anything else made me less confident in my faith. I thought about how I was once afraid to walk away from people who didn't treat me like the true Christian I could be. Like the Miss Righteous I should be.

Just before I drifted off to sleep, I thanked God for bringing Hunter into my life. He wasn't my Mr. Righteous, but it meant the world to know that a man like him existed. He often questioned why someone as experienced in the political world as me would take the time to mentor and talk to him. He didn't feel like we were equals. The truth was, he was the first righteous man to ever make me feel like I could be his equal.

I also thanked God for His forgiveness and patience with me. Even in my darkest moments of defiance, He didn't leave me. He showed me who I should be and that my focus should be on Him. When I put God in the forefront so many of my insecurities and anxieties about men seemed to fall away.

The next morning, I remembered the first article I ever had published. It was a movie review when I was fourteen. It was the first of a biweekly column in the city paper. I immediately called Hunter.

"Have you ever seen the movie about the country singer who leaves in the middle of a concert?" I asked.

"I know where this is going," he said.

"No, you don't," I said.

"OK, what?"

"So, the main character's name was Hunter, obviously."

"Obviously," he said back to me.

"Well, that means my first-ever published article was about a Hunter!" I said excitedly.

"See, our friendship was meant to be!" he said.

Blessed be the one who took notice of you. — *Ruth 2:19*

ACKNOWLEDGMENTS

Whenever I am tempted to lose patience with God and with the obstacles in life, I try to remember how patient He has been with me. I am thankful to Him for salvation and guidance as I told this story.

Here on Earth, I thank my family for their love and support— my parents (Richard, Judy, and Mark) and my sister, Jennifer. Thank you for being my biggest fans.

I am especially grateful for my friends who read early editions of this book and endured my ups and downs in person—Jimmie Bise, Christie Herrera, Jimmy LaSalvia, Joseph Logue, Liz Neaton, Lesli Phelps, Floyd Resnick, and Dustin Schluterman. Special thanks also to Pat Neaton for his helpful advice on legal matters beyond my comprehension.

Thank you to the mentors who have encouraged me in my writing and faith—Ann Coulter, Jen Lancaster, Eric Metaxas, and Elizabeth Sheld. They are the embodiment of the great people Mark Twain had in mind when he said, "Keep away from people who try to belittle your ambitions. Small people always do that, but the really great make you feel that you, too, can become great."

Finally, sincere thanks to my agent, Jennifer Cohen, Post Hill Press, and my publicist, Dave Mohel at Blue Skin Solutions, for believing in this book.